Taking Back THE NIGHT

Restoring God's Season Of Power In This Present Darkness

Paula Matthews

Spirit & Life
Publications^{SM}

In Memory
Of
Apostle Frederick K. C. Price III
(January 3, 1932 - February 12, 2021)

My Pastor and Spiritual Father,
Who taught me, both through his coaching and his example,
How to stand in faith in the midst of great adversity.
I pray that I've learned the lessons well.

Taking Back The Night
Restoring God's Season Of Power
In This Present Darkness
Copyright ©2020 Paula Matthews

All rights reserved. No part of this book may be
Reproduced in any form by any electronic or
Mechanical means including photocopying, recording,
Or information storage and retrieval without written
Permission from the author.

Unless otherwise noted, scripture quotations are from
The Holy Bible: Authorized
King James Version,
©2003 Thomas Nelson, Inc.

Printed in the United States Of America

ISBN: 978-1-7357642-4-5

Spirit & Life
Publications℠
Ɛ

www.spiritandlifepublications.com
Atlanta

Contents

PROPHETIC WARNING!

AUTHOR'S NOTE
The Purpose For Planet Earth: The Director's Cut   13

INTRODUCTION
And God Saw That Light Was Good   21
God Called The Light DAY And The Darkness NIGHT   33
Walking Through The Shadows   45

TAKING DOMINION OVER THE NIGHT
Treading Over All Enemy Powers   61
Knowing Our God And His Covenant   79
Discerning Truth From Lies   91
Waging A Warfare   113

CONCLUSION
Experience Good In The Land Of The Living   133
Life Or Death: It's A Matter Of Choice   147

BIBLIOGRAPHY

PROPHETIC WARNING!

Throughout Bible history, God has sent His word (Truth) to deliver, exhort, chastise and warn, His people, and the kings who have been anointed to rule over them. In those days, God revealed His Truth through His holy prophets. In these last days, He has revealed His Truth through His Son Jesus Christ. Today, God's Truth is still being revealed through the Sons of God, who are led by the Spirit of God in this earth. The spirit behind all divine prophecy is the revelation of Jesus Christ, His person, plan and purpose for the earth (Revelation 19:10).

The Lord has declared by His Spirit, that we have entered into a **"new era"** in which **"the wisdom of men is over."** God is taking back the earth, its people and possessions for His Kingdom purpose. Therefore, whatever is not of God, will collapse and fail in this era. **"It shall not stand."**

We are in the time that the Prophet Daniel saw, where God is raising up His Kingdom in the earth, and it shall destroy all other kingdoms. God's Kingdom will not be left to other rulers, for He alone is the King Eternal, and His Kingdom shall stand forever (Daniel 2:44). Therefore, every nation and kingdom under heaven must align itself with God's Kingdom agenda, if it is to survive.

Our times and seasons are in God's Hand. He created us and chose us for such a time as this. We all have a role to play in what He calls **<u>His</u> "Grand Finale before Jesus returns."** These days will be **"explosive"** with God's supernatural power. Each of us must make sure that we are on the **"right side"** of that explosion, if we want to live and see good days in the land of the living.

Paula Matthews
Kingdom Apostle,
Prophetess and Daughter of the Most High God

*"There are many devices in a man's heart;
Nevertheless the Counsel of The Lord,
<u>That</u> shall stand "*
       Proverbs 19:21

AUTHOR'S NOTE
The Purpose For Planet Earth: The Director's Cut

God's purpose for earth can be summed up in a few simple words. *"Thy kingdom come. Thy will be done in earth, as it is in heaven* (Matthew 6:10)." Jesus told us to pray these words daily. This was God's original intent for earth, to be a reflection, the very essence and glory of Heaven, with the power and glory of God operating in the lives of mankind, providing all that we need to thrive for all eternity. This was God's good plan for mankind. Everything God created was *very good* (Genesis 1:31). He created it for our good, because His thoughts toward us are only *for good and not evil* (Jeremiah 29:11). Now, take a look around the earth today. Everything is in a mess. God didn't plan this. He didn't defile the earth. Mankind did, and we have no solution that can clean up this mess. God alone, saw this day, and prepared a solution for mankind. That is why we pray, to find God's answers for earth. This is also why we must pray for God's Kingdom to come. We want to see His *good* will done on earth, as it is in Heaven.

We need God. We need His Kingdom solutions to be in operation upon the earth. For that to happen, God needs is a man, a family, a people who are willing to do His will on earth. Adam, the son of God, was created for such a purpose, but he departed from God to do his own thing. Officially, Adam was appointed as earth's first and only king. His throne was established in righteousness, but this son of God chose to erect his own throne in opposition to that of his Father, God. Now, many preachers focus on how the serpent beguiled the Eve and caused the man to turn against God. This is true, however, this is not how God never blamed the woman or the serpent for treason. God faults King Adam, who abdicated his throne causing the entire earth to be bound to the curse of sin and death. Another kingdom system arose in the earth. One of established in unrighteousness, upon *"the lust of the flesh, and the lust of the eyes, and the pride of life."* These things were not of the Father, but of the world. Unfortunately, Adam's curse, would extend to this new "world system," and the kingdoms therein. All would be cursed to fail, and men to die. The kingdoms of this world would pass away along with the lusts there of (I John 2:16-17). God's Kingdom was established to reign forever. His plan was for mankind to experience righteousness for all eternity. This *Eternal Life* was God's original idea from the beginning. Those who do the will of God would abide with Him forever. Those who follow after the world would be eternally separated from God. The story of earth is, a **"Tale of Two Kingdom Systems"** battling for the souls of men. It's Man versus God, a battle that began with the Father's desire for an earthly family. It began when God made Adam.

God's original plan, was for His family to rule upon the earth as righteous kings. After Adam fell, Jesus was sent into the world to reestablish God's Kingdom order, and legacy of righteous kings. God appointed Jesus as King over the Kingdom (Colossians 1:13). Even before Jesus was born, it had been prophesied that God would raise a Kingdom on earth, *"which shall never be destroyed: and the kingdom shall not be left to other people, [but] it shall break in pieces and consume all these kingdoms, and it shall stand for ever* (Daniel 2:44)." In the Bible, we see God's Kingdom raised in the beginning (Genesis 1-2). At the very end of time, we who are live with Christ, will see the Kingdom fully restored and reigning on the earth once again (Revelation 21-22).

In the meantime, the battle between the **"two kingdom systems"** remains. God continues to search for a man [or woman] to lead the nations in righteousness, while wicked men vie for earthly kingdoms to fulfill their lust for power. The saints of God are forever praying, *"Thy Kingdom come. Thy will be done."* After centuries of God's saints praying these words, the Kingdom is manifesting in increased measure. God's Kingdom has invaded the earth. It didn't start in our lifetime. It started when John the Baptist came preaching, *"Repent, for the Kingdom of Heaven is at hand* (Matthew 3:2)." Then Jesus came preaching the Kingdom (Matthew 4:17), preparing the world for His return to set up His earthly throne. Today, earth has embarked upon a **"new era."** Life as we know it is over. We are at **"the end of the last days,"** a time for the restoration of all things before Jesus Christ returns (Acts 3:21). God created this earth for His purpose, and in this **"new era,"** He will be **"taking everything back under His government rule."** God's Kingdom is in **"rapid recovery mode."** The earth, it's people and possessions must be restored back to God's original purpose and intent. According to the Holy Spirit, God is about to reveal **"The Director's Cut"** upon the planet earth. We are all familiar with this term as it applies to movies and film. It is a special release of a film that honors the director's original intent. Often the studio determines which version of a film is released. The director does not always have the opportunity to produce his or her original version with narration explaining why they chose to emphasize certain aspects of the film in the way they did. In the earth, God is about to tell the tale in His own *powerful* way. Here is *some* of what to expect.

Consider planet Earth. God created it with His own purpose in mind, but when He gave mankind dominion, the version of this planet we see now, is not what God intended. Jesus left the Church in charge to demonstrate God's Kingdom operation throughout the world. However, most of what has been displayed is religion. God hates religion. It is not from Him. Religion is a product of the curse. Religion is a kingdom that has been raised in the earth to war against God's Kingdom. It's purpose is to pervert the true meaning of Christianity. For the record, God would like the world to know that **"Christianity is not a religion. It is a Kingdom way of living, of sharing and loving our fellow man."** **Period.**

Here is the problem, according to the script (the Bible) it is almost time for Jesus to make **"His grand entrance on the world stage"** as King of kings and Lord of lords, <u>but</u> the Church nor the world is prepared for such a dramatic appearance. Jesus said, that there would be tribulations, wars and pestilences and earthquakes as a sign of His return, but these are just the "beginning of sorrows." All of these things were prophesied to happen, but Jesus also said that *"this gospel of the Kingdom shall be preached,"* and then the end would come.

There are Christians who are crying out for the end to come, but the gospel of the Kingdom has yet to be preached. Many Christians have no idea of what God's Kingdom is, or how it operates. Jesus <u>will not</u> return, nor can He, until the Kingdom is demonstrated in every sector of this world. Therefore, God has to **"flip the script"** on a rebellious Church. They are about to become part of God's Kingdom demonstration, and it won't be pretty. God is about to demonstrate His original intent for earth in a **"highly dramatic fashion"** that will **"stun"** the world. Here is the prophecy the Lord gave me:

"I am God. I change not. I set the stage. I choose the actors.
Those who didn't like the part, I have changed.
The performance date has been set, the venue chosen.
It's time to take center stage in this,
My Grand Finale before My Son returns."
"This is it! Take your places now!"
Says, The Faithful God,
Director of it all![1]

Some prophets have called this a **"global reset."** All I know is that the Lord said that **"Righteousness will prevail on earth"** in this **"new era."** How is this possible when unrighteousness appears to be ruling and reigning throughout the earth, even in America where God has a covenant with that land? Consider the fact, that this is not the first time God placed a **"reset"** in the earth. Let's go back to the beginning, to creation. *"In the beginning God created the heaven and the earth* (Genesis 1:1)." Something happened in the earth, after God created it because the next verse says, *"And the earth was without form, and void; and darkness was upon the face of the deep* (Genesis 1:2)." How is possible for God to create the heavens and earth at one point in time, and discover it destroyed in yet another point in time? What happened to earth? Jesus gives us a hint when He said, *"I beheld Satan as lightning fall from heaven* (Luke 10:18)." More of the story is revealed in the Book of Revelation. When it tells of a rebellion in Heaven in which Lucifer (Satan, the devil) is cast down to earth in exile (Revelation 12:7-17). Jesus said the devil fell like lightning

---

1   Matthews, Paula. "Birth Pains Of The Sons Of God." *The War Journal (2011-2020) Volume III*. Atlanta: Spirit & Life Publications[SM], 2020. 102. Print.

upon the earth. Could this rebellion in Heaven have resulted in the destruction of earth? We can't prove what happened, but the Bible describes how the earth went through a **"reset"** in Genesis 1:2-31. Afterwards, there was a new heavens and a new earth.

There was yet another time in which there was a **"reset"** in the earth. It happened during the days of Noah. Here is what the Bible says. *"And GOD saw that the wickedness of man [was] great in the earth, and [that] every imagination of the thoughts of his heart [was] only evil continually. And it repented the LORD that he had made man on the earth, and it grieved him at his heart. And the LORD said, I will destroy man whom I have created from the face of the earth; both man, and beast, and the creeping thing, and the fowls of the air; for it repenteth me that I have made them* (Genesis 6:5-7)." You know the story. God had Noah build an ark to preserve them from the deluge of water that was coming upon the earth. Noah preached about the coming flood and the people refused to listen, until the rain came. Then it was too late, and they perished. This was God's judgment against the wickedness of mankind. Every living thing outside of that ark perished. God re-populated the earth with Noah and his sons. Can you say **"global reset?"**

There is one common theme in these stories. No matter what mankind plotted or schemed, it always failed, proving that "*the counsel [plans and purpose] of the Lord*" shall stand (Proverbs 19:21). So, what can we expect in this **"new era?"** Here is another clue. Jesus said that before He returns, our days would be like those in the days of Noah. *"For as in the days that were before the flood they were eating and drinking, marrying and giving in marriage, until the day that Noe entered into the ark, And knew not until the flood came, and took them all away; so shall also the coming of the Son of man be* (Matthew 24:38-39)." Just like Noah preached about the flood coming and the people refused to listen and perish, so shall it be in our day. The end time prophets are preaching the Kingdom and many will not hear until it's too late. This is all part of what God calls **"His Grand Finale"** before Jesus returns. What can we expect in this final chapter of earth, *"the final reset?"* Here is a prophecy from Heaven. ***"This coming move of God is His Grand Finale before Jesus comes; Fire in the Sky and Earth; Fireworks. It's the time of God's justice; good and bad rewarded f their persistence."***[2] This grand finale will be a time of God's justice. *"Fire!" "Fireworks!"* It all sounds explosive. It's what anyone would expect from a grand finale. It will be a good time for some and a not so good time for others. One thing is for sure, after the flood of Noah's day, God *"reset"* the earth with a new covenant. The rainbow is the symbol of God's covenant that He will not destroy us again by water (Genesis 9:14-15). That's good news, but what judgement is reserved for this era will be far greater than water. Here is what the Bible says. *"But the day of the Lord will come as a thief in the night; in the which the heavens shall pass away with a great noise, and the elements shall melt with fervent heat, the earth also and the works that are therein shall be burned up* (II Peter 3:10)." The earth burned up? The writer of Hebrews exhorts us to receive the Kingdom. *"For our God is a consuming fire* (Hebrews 12:29)." God will indeed send His fire upon the earth. And why not? If God is going to *"shake"* rebellious men into righteousness, it will take fire. That is what God is promising in this *"**His Grand Finale.**"* God is bringing His Fire to the earth to consume the wicked and purify His people, all of this to prepare for the new heavens and the new earth to come, where there will be only righteousness (II Peter 3:13).

Let's explore *"**The Director's Cut**"* a bit further. Men on earth believe that they are "free moral agents" to do as they please. Sure, we can do as we please, but if our will goes against the will of God, we end up in the curse. That's not where God wants us to live. God gave mankind dominion to be Blessed. This is *"**righteous dominion**"* that comes from obedience to God's will and purpose. *"And God blessed them, and God said unto them, Be fruitful, and multiply, and replenish the earth, and subdue it, and have dominion . . . (Genesis 1:28)."* The Blessing established God's *"**divine partnership**"* with mankind for the wellbeing of the earth. Human beings were not created to oper-

---

[2] Matthews, Paula. "Year 2002: *The Enemy Exposed & God's Plan Revealed.*" *The War Journal (1999-2010) Volume I.* Los Angeles: Spirit & Life Publications, 2010. 181. Print.

ate without God. Man's breath (life) came directly from God (Genesis 2:7). It was that Breath of God (Holy Spirit) that made man a living soul like his Father. **"Mankind was created to work in concert with His Maker and Father God."** He gave us the Blessing in which to rule over this earth by increasing it's fruitfulness, replenishing whatever would be lacking and subduing every enemy that would come against earth and its inhabitants. This is a far cry from what we see in the world today. Mankind still has dominion, but it is wicked and unrighteous, yet God has not given up on us. That is why He sent Jesus to show us *"the way."* That is why He gave us the Holy Spirit to help and guide along *"the way"* of life. In a world that is full of lies and deception (darkness), God loved us to much to give us the Spirit of Truth (*Light*) to show us things to come (John 16:13). The Holy Spirit is our covenant partner. He helps us fulfill God's will for our lives. He shows us how to be the *light* in the midst of the darkness of this world. Make no mistake about it, every human on earth was created to partner with God **"to make a difference in the world."** Not all have agreed to do so. They follow the way of the curse like their father Adam and do their own thing in this earth without God. Consequently, mankind has been fruitful in the curse which has caused the world to experience lack, unable to replenish itself, and at the mercy of the evil one.

God sent His son Jesus Christ to give us back righteous dominion, but many have refused. We now find ourselves in a **"kairos moment in time,"** God's appointed season to do all of His will. He is taking the earth and it's people back **"on script."** The Holy Spirit said that **"the works of man has ended . . . righteousness returns to the earth."** This was spoken of in the prophecy. The earth is full of darkness, yet God's Glory is arising upon His people. We will be the *light* that will lead people out of darkness. Consider what is happening in the earth today? There are wars and rumors of wars throughout the world and in the United States. It would seem that darkness is prevailing, but God has commanded that **"Darkness shall not prevail."** God has spoken, even as the evil one refuses to relent. This is also according to script. According to the prophecy, God set the stage and chose the actors. Scripture also confirms that the Lord made all things for Himself, even the wicked for the day of evil (Proverbs 16:4). In fact, God made *"of one blood all nations of men for to dwell on all the face of the earth, and hath determined the times before appointed, and the bounds of their habitation* (Acts 17:26)." If you are among the living, then God has purposed for you to be here for such a time as this. There is a specific purpose you are to complete before Jesus returns.

In these last days, darkness may refuse to back down, but God has declared this to be a season of His **"*justice.*"** He will show His wrath and make His power known to the world. The Lord will also prove that He is able to deliver the godly in the evil day, not only deliver them, but also prosper them profusely. God will **"*work wonders*"** through His **"*faithful*"** servants. **"*This is God's chosen season to work His will in the lives of His people, for His purpose alone!*"** God will show Himself strong on behalf of His covenant people. In this **"*new era*"** there will be a **"*marked distinction*"** between that which is holy (set aside for God's purpose) and that which is unholy; between that which God considers good versus that which the Father says is evil.

Righteousness shall prevail in these last days before Jesus returns. According to God, **"*Earth is back on script. There will be no turning back.*"** The government of God is taking back the earth, and the devil knows that Jesus is headed this way. The spirit of Antichrist is on the rise even in America. That means the evil day (the Night) is coming to an **"*explosive*"** end. Satan and his demons are resisting in an attempt to stop the Lord from taking it all back, but it is useless. God is **"*unstoppable.*"** Ultimately God will have His way with or without our cooperation. It is the goodness of God that He allows us to participate in His will. Thankfully, God has a faithful people in the earth. The Lord will uphold His covenant for the sake of this **"*handful*"** of believers who trust Him. They will release the **"*goodness*"** of our God in the land of the living. They will make God and His son Jesus Christ **"*famous*"** in all the earth!

INTRODUCTION

And God Saw That Light Was Good

When the earth was in darkness, without form and void. God said, *"Let there be light: and there was light."* God encountered the darkness of this world, by calling forth *light*. God saw that the *light* was good. The *Light* was good because it illuminated the earth. It made clear that which had been hidden in darkness.

Next, the Bible says that God *divided [separated, distinguished]*, the *light* from the darkness. Somehow, *light came out of the darkness*, which implies that the *light* and the darkness were joined. This got me thinking, "How could light come from darkness?" This led to other questions. "Which came first, the *light* or the darkness?" The Holy Spirit began calling to my mind scriptures like 1 John 1:5 which says, *"God is light, and in him is no darkness at all."* Therefore as scripture shows the *Light* (God) had to come first, if God was the Creator of it all. Also God could only create from that which was in Him, that being only *light*. It was not in Him to create darkness.

God (*Light*) was first. We now know why *light* was good. Jesus said that *"there is none good but God* (Matthew 19:17)." God came first and God is good. Everything God created was also full of *light* (glory). Everything God created was also good. Hold onto those two thoughts. If this is true about God and His creation, where did the darkness come from? We mentioned the war in Heaven in which Lucifer (satan, devil) was cast down to earth in exile. Jesus witnessed him falling from Heaven (Luke 10:18). This would have been no ordinary lightning to be able to destroy God's creation, leaving the earth in darkness without form and void. The Bible gives no details of how the earth became in the evil state. All we know is that God called forth the *light* which had already been there, but had been blocked by the darkness. This is very significant because whatever God does in this earth, it is to divide the *light* from the darkness; to open the eyes of mankind and redeem them from the power of darkness and translate them into the Kingdom of *Light*. God calls us out of the darkness of this world. Those who answer the call, are called the "children"of *Light*. According to scripture, God *"chose us in Him before the foundation of the world* (Ephesians 1:4)." We all are spirits that came from God. He knew us before we were in our mother's womb (Jeremiah 1:5). When our time came to be reunited with our Father, He called us forth out of the darkness of this world, just like He did all creation. What a Mighty God He is!

Indeed, Almighty God is **"The Director Of It All."** Truth be known, God is **"The Producer, Writer and Director Of It All!"** Almighty God conceived us in His Heart before the worlds were formed. *Light* came first indeed. The *Light* of God was first in our lives. He knew each of us before we were born. Each and every human being on the planet had knowledge of *Light* before coming into this world. He sent Jesus (the Light of the World) to restore us back to the Father, so that we too could be the *light* of God in this world. *"For whom he did foreknow, he also did predestinate [to be] conformed to the image of his Son, that he might be the firstborn among many brethren* (Romans 8:29)."

God pre-knew and predestined us, but when we entered into the darkness of this world, *light* was hidden from us. Our eyes were blinded by the evil one, our minds conformed to the darkness of this world until we would experience *light* once again. This is why the preaching of the gospel is vital to the lives of men on earth. The world needs Jesus. As the Bible says, *"In Him was life; and the life was the light of men* (John 1:4)." Jesus came to earth saying that He was the Way, the Truth and the Life. No man can return to God except by Him (John 14:6). Jesus was sent by the Father to lead us back home, not to an earthly home, but back to our Heavenly Father's household. Not all have returned to God. They remain lost, ignoring the gospel of truth. *"But if our gospel be hid, it is hid to them that are lost: In whom the god of this world hath blinded the minds of them which believe not, lest the light of the glorious gospel of Christ, who is the image of God, should shine unto them* (II Corinthians 4:3-4)."

God definitely saw that *light* was good. It reconciled us back to our Heavenly Father, and called us with a holy calling, *"not according to our works, but according to his own purpose and grace, which was given us in Christ Jesus before the world began* (II Timothy 1:9)." We are spirits on a mission. Most of the world knows that God sent Jesus on a mission to save us. Not many realize that once saved, we have been given the same mission. God said to me, **"Paula, be!"** He had called me forth out of darkness when I got saved some thirty years prior, never knowing that God had a purpose for my life. In church all my life, and I never heard that God had an assignment for me. It was never taught. Having read through the Bible several times, I never saw it in the scriptures. My mind was blinded by religion. I went to church every Sunday, yet living like those in the world. I worked in the ministry and the *light* never came to me, until tragedy struck.

Life blindsided me and I began to cry out to God in my suffering. My life was in crisis and God responded not with sympathy, but with judgment. He boldly let me know that **"first and foremost, I belonged to Him!"** My life was out of order with Him. I was God's child. I had no right to live life as I pleased. I repented for my ignorance about my responsibility to God. How was I to know? It was never taught. God called me out of Egypt (the world) for His Kingdom service. His *light* shined into my darkness and illuminated my assignment and call. For the first time, my eyes were opened and the scripture that says, *"But ye are a chosen generation, a royal priesthood, an holy nation, a peculiar people; that ye should shew forth the praises of him who hath called you out of darkness into his marvellous light* (I Peter 2:9)."

What I love about God, is that there is no level of darkness where He cannot reach you. The Psalmist David wrote, *"If I say, Surely the darkness shall cover me; even the night shall be light about me. Yea, the darkness hideth not from thee; but the night shineth as the day: the darkness and the light [are] both alike [to thee]. For thou hast possessed my reins: thou hast covered me in my mother's womb. I will praise thee; for I am fearfully [and] wonderfully made: marvellous [are] thy works; and [that] my soul knoweth right well* (Psalm 139:11-14)."

Until we are redeemed back to God we will continue to live our lives in darkness, not only in sin, but also in ignorance about our God and His purpose for life. God anticipated that we would be that way, so He gave us His word to live by. *"The entrance of thy words giveth light; it giveth understanding unto the simple* (Psalm 119:130)." God's word gives us *light*, which means clarity and understanding as concerns His divine plan and purpose. Not everyone wants the *light*. Jesus said, *"And this is the condemnation, that light is come into the world, and men loved darkness rather than light, because their deeds were evil* (John 3:19)." Evil men won't come to the *light*. They want to stay hidden in darkness. As a result, there are two types of people in the world, those who come to the light and those who remain in darkness. God intentionally makes a difference between the children of *Light* and the children of darkness. It's His way of advertising or promoting the goodness of His Kingdom to the nations of the earth. As the Bible says, it is the goodness of God that leads men to repentance (Romans 2:4). The true purpose of *light* is to lead us to back to God and His original purpose, which is to shower us with His goodness.

We can find God's original intent by going back to the beginning. The Bible says that *"God saw every thing that He had made, and, behold, it was very good* (Genesis 1:31)." So, if everything God made was good, where did evil come from? This was the question I asked in Sunday School as a teenager. If God only does good, where does evil come? The teacher didn't have an answer. Today I know the answer to that question. Evil came about when sin entered the world. Sin happened when Adam turned his back on God and decided to do his own thing. He was ignorant of the fact that mankind was never created to operate on our own. This was my problem. I thought that we were created to live our own lives. Even as a Christian, God was not in any of my thoughts when it came to everyday life. Like Adam, I was unaware of my purpose. Never would I have known that it was far greater than my satisfying my own desires on earth. Like Adam, my purpose involved not only me, but my family, my city, state, nation, and ultimately all of the people of the earth. My greatest awakening was to realize that my life was not all about me.

My life was full of darkness, not knowing the glory. Adam was filled with the *light* (glory) of God. He was surrounded by *light*, and yet he could not see what God had given him. The same is true of people in our day. Many of us have been told that salvation has to do with leaving the darkness of this world and going to Heaven. Therefore we live in this earth as though we have no other purpose than to withstand evil and suffer until Jesus comes. We have come into the *light*, but unable to see truth. This brings us to **another aspect of the darkness that involves God hiding truth for His people to discover.** We find that the more *light* we walk in, the more *light* God reveals to us. *"For whosoever hath, to him shall be given, and he shall have more abundance: but whosoever hath not, from him shall be taken away even that he hath* (Matthew 13:12)." This is what happened to me. The more God revealed, the more I began to follow. The more I followed Him, the more He revealed of what was hidden in Christ for my life.

God's Kingdom has many treasures for us that have been hidden in a mystery. Salvation is more than forgiveness of sins. God has an inheritance for us in the earth. In fact, the only reason sin is an issue is because it prevents us from obtaining our divine inheritance. God revealed to me that as His children, we have an inheritance. *"The Spirit itself beareth witness with our spirit, that we are the children of God: And if children, then heirs; heirs of God, and joint-heirs with Christ* (Romans 8:17)*"* of everything that belongs to God. As the scripture says, *"The earth is the Lord's, and the fullness thereof: the world, and they that dwell therein* (Psalm 24:1)." Everything in earth belongs to God and His heirs. *"Ask of me, and I shall give [thee] the heathen [for] thine inheritance, and the uttermost parts of the earth [for] thy possession* (Psalm 2:8).*"* God has made us heirs of this world. This is the *light* that the rulers of the darkness of this world don't want us to know. The devil wants to keep us blinded about our identity in Christ so that we would never walk in our earthly inheritances. God has purposed that we should obtain our inheritance, even before Jesus returns. There is land that must be claimed by the people of God in this **"new era."** We have an inheritance in the land.

This earth was created for God's kids. It all belongs to Him, yet the Father has given it to us for a specific purpose. Whether we realize it or not, there is longing for purpose in every human heart. God placed it within us. King Solomon wrote that God placed eternity in the hearts of men so *"that no man can find out the work that God maketh from the beginning to the end* (Ecclesiastes 3:11)." It's true that so much about God's plans are shrouded in a mystery far out of reach of human knowledge and manipulation. This is also where God hides His treasures for His people. *"And I will give thee the treasures of darkness, and hidden riches of secret places, that thou mayest know that I, the LORD, which call [thee] by thy name, [am] the God of Israel* (Isaiah 45:3)." Again we can quote Solomon who said, *"[It is] the glory of God to conceal a thing: but the honour of kings [is] to search out a matter* (Proverbs 25:2)." It's the nature and honor of God to hide His precious things in a mystery. It's our honor as kings and queens of His Kingdom to search out those hidden things. It pleases the Father when we pursue Him and His mysteries.

Even the fulness of our salvation is hidden inside the heart of the believer. God hides His glory within His people. The Bible says, *"To whom God would make known what [is] the riches of the glory of this mystery among the Gentiles; which is Christ in you, the hope of glory* (Colossians 1:27)." God and His *light* is within us. *"For God, who commanded the light to shine out of darkness, hath shined in our hearts, to [give] the light of the knowledge of the glory of God in the face of Jesus Christ. But we have this treasure in earthen vessels, that the excellency of the power may be of God, and not of us* (II Corinthians 4:6-7)."

The Bible says that the *"secret things"* belong to God, but what He reveals to His people is our inheritance forever (Deuteronomy 29:29). It all begins with the word that God speaks to our hearts. These revelations from God are *the light* that shineth in the darkness of this world. It is the lamp to our feet and the *light* of our path in life (Psalm 119:105). God's revelation is downloaded to our spirits by the Holy Spirit (I Corinthians 2:10). It is **"the script"** for our lives that leads us to the Father's preordained destiny and purpose for our lives.

Solomon wrote that there is *"a season and a time to every purpose"* under God's Heaven (Ecclesiastes 3:1). There is also a season and time for *every person* under Heaven. There are no accidents with God. Everything and everyone on earth has been predestined by God for a specific purpose. As individuals, our central focus in life should be to discover and fulfill our God given purpose. That purpose doesn't just fall out of the sky. It is also not as obvious as one would think. When God called me into public ministry, **"the script"** from Heaven was downloaded in my heart by the Holy Spirit. It was a shock and an awe! There was no way I could have ever thought to do any of the things the Lord had for me to do. Everything looked impossible. In fact, everything He showed me was impossible. That's how I knew it had to be a dream from God. My mind had to be renewed, just to be able to receive what God showed me. I recall standing in the kitchen of my cousin's house in Los Angeles when God first talked to me about His call upon my life. We had just come back home after church. I walked into the kitchen and the Lord flashed a *vision* of me standing behind a pulpit, preaching. I had a fit, a royal temper tantrum. It took me three days to calm down enough to accept what the Lord was showing me. My cousin wanted me to hurry up and make things right with God, for fear that He would strike her house with lightning.

Then the Lord had me study the Book of Ephesians and more *light* was shed in my heart. The Lord showed me how the purpose for my life was intertwined with that of the Church, my nation and the world. It was an honor for God to allow me to help Him carry out the Kingdom mission in this earth. Today, I can honestly say that following God was the best decision I've ever made. There is great satisfaction in knowing that you are in the will of God for your life. There is nothing like it in this world. God had a great purpose for my life; like He does for every human being. Jesus came and died to restore the earth, its inhabitants and possessions back to the Father. Within that restoration lies the reconciliation of our families and our nations. Christians are taught about reconciling the souls of men back to God. Very little is spoken about reconciling the nations of the earth. His vision for mankind is **"global."** From the beginning, Adam and Eve were Blessed to be fruitful and multiply, to the populate the whole earth. Adam named his wife Eve because she was to be the mother of *all living beings* (Genesis 3:20). After the flood during Noah's days, Noah and His sons and their families were saved from destruction in order to *re-populate the nations* of earth after the deluge (Genesis 10:32). God's heart has always been for the nations of the earth. His desire is to bring forth nations through us. Take the story of Abraham. He was old and his wife Sarah was well beyond childbearing years. God promised them a son, but that promise did not end there. God said to Abraham that many nations would come from his loins. *"Behold my covenant is with thee, and thou shalt be a father of many nations* (Genesis 17:4)." The same promise was seen in Isaac, the son of Abraham. When Isaac's wife Rebekah became pregnant with twins, there was a struggle going on inside of her womb. She inquired of the Lord. *"And the LORD said unto her, Two nations [are] in thy womb, and two manner of people shall be separated from thy bowels; and [the one] people shall be stronger than [the other] people; and the elder shall serve the younger* (Genesis 25:23)." Then we saw this promise again with Isaac's son Jacob, who was also the grandson of Abraham. Jacob had twelve sons who began as twelves tribes, and later would become the nation of Israel.

God said to Abraham, *"And I will make thy seed to multiply as the stars of heaven, and will give unto thy seed all these countries; and in thy seed shall all the nations of the earth be blessed* (Genesis 26:4)." This was God's promise to the natural sons of Abraham, and yet it did not end there either. The Bible says that if we are in Christ, then we are Abraham's seed, and heirs of that same promise (Galatians 3:29). This is far beyond the normal idea of what it means to be Christian. It's not only about us and our families and communities. It is about being Blessed to bless all the families of the earth. It's about possessing people and lands for the Kingdom inheritance. *"I will declare the decree: the Lord hath said unto me, Thou art my son; this day have I begotten thee. Ask of me, and I shall give [thee] the heathen [for] thine inheritance, and the uttermost parts of the earth [for] thy pos-*

session.(Psalm 2:7-8).*"* This is God's ultimate purpose for the earth, to reconcile mankind back to His original purpose so that we can receive an earthly inheritance. The traditional Church has taught that the gospel message is about sin, but the Bible clearly shows that it has and continues to be about God looking for a family in the earth. In short, salvation is about more than going to Heaven. It is about bringing Heaven down to the earth. It is about the sons of God ruling and reigning in the Name of Jesus in the earth. In other words, what God has in mind for our salvation, is far greater than anything we could ever imagine. As the Bible says, that God *"is able to do exceeding abundantly above all that we ask or think, according to the power that worketh in us* (Ephesians 3:20).*"*

I recall a *vision* from the Lord that brought this idea home to me. *In this vision, I saw books entitled, Matthew, Mark, Luke, John and The Book of Acts on a book shelf. Then I saw another book entitled,* **"The Last Book of Acts."** *That book flew off the book shelf and pages opened to a chapter in which my name and my company EPIC Ventures, was mentioned in that book. My purpose was included in The Last Book Of Acts and it included great works for the Kingdom worldwide.* Sure, my assignment was included in the Acts of the last Apostles, but the Lord had shown my company in the Bible, years prior to that *vision*. My assignment and call was a mystery shrouded in darkness (ignorance) The *Light* of God through the Holy Spirit illuminated the scriptures and the Lord called forth my company out of Ephesians 3:10-11. *"To the intent that now unto the principalities and powers in heavenly [places] might be known by the church the manifold wisdom of God, According to the **E**ternal **P**urpose which he purposed **I**n **C**hrist Jesus our Lord* (Ephesians 3:10-11).*"* The Holy Spirit highlighted Eternal Purpose In Christ (EPIC). From the pages of scripture the Lord began talking about what this company would do worldwide. Then He said, **"This is just the beginning."** For years, the Lord had me calling forth EPIC Ventures and it's associated companies. I called them forth out of the darkness (obscurity) into the *light* of day. All I needed to bring God's *vision* to pass, was faith the size of a mustard seed, and a willingness to hold fast to my faith until it is fully manifested.

Beloved, if what you are believing for is the will of God for your life, then go forth in mustard seed of faith. Be consistent in your faith and watch how it will grow and become greater than you ever imagined. It is designed to bless and provide for the welfare of many lives in the earth. I exhort you, not to despise small beginnings (Zechariah 4:10). God starts with something that seems small, but ultimate His goal is to reach all the nations of the earth. That's how it was with Adam. That's how it was with Abraham and that is how it is with everyone who is a member of God's family through Jesus Christ. Our assignment is bigger than us. It involves not only people, but the earth and it's possessions. We are about to manifest this in a greater *light* in these last days of darkness.

As the greater *lights* in the world, we are simply stewards of God's property. We are caretakers of the earth and its possessions. When God created Adam, he was placed in the garden to *"dress and keep it* (Genesis 2:15)."* It was also amazing that the Lord brought every animal to Adam *"to see what he would call them* (Genesis 2:19)."* How did Adam know what to call animals he had never seen before? Where did he get the names? Isaiah gives us a clue. *"I have put my words in they mouth, and I have covered thee in the shadow of mine hand, that I may plant the heavens and lay the foundations of the earth* (Isaiah 51:16)." The Lord told Jeremiah, *"Behold, I have put my words in thy mouth. See, I have this day set thee over the nations and over the kingdoms, to root out, and to pull down, and to destroy, and to throw down, to build, and to plant* (Jeremiah 1:9-10)." Darkness may surround us in this world, but we are called to imitate our Heavenly Father (Ephesians 5:1), by opening our mouths and calling forth the *light*. As people of God, we are ordained to speak solutions to the issues of this world. For example, Jesus said that before He returned to the earth, that nations would rise against nation, and kingdom against kingdom. The devil knows his time is short, therefore he is causing all kinds of trouble inciting wars and disseminating rumors of wars among the nations (Matthew 24:6-7). The nations and the kingdoms of this earth are shaking even now at the *light* of God's word that says, *"The kingdoms of this world are become [the kingdoms] of our*

Lord, and of his Christ; and he shall reign for ever and ever (Revelation 11:15)." The rulers of darkness refuse to relinquish their control over the earth, but they cannot stop God's word from going forth. Their only recourse is to create chaos and deception, by attempting to steal, kill and destroy that which belongs to God, both the people and possessions. The *light* is overtaking the darkness and nothing can stop it from happening. *"And the light shineth in darkness' and the darkness comprehended it not* (John 1:5)."

Jesus warned that there would be *"famines, and pestilences, and earthquakes in divers places* (Matthew 24:7)." Even the earth is in sync with the *light* of God's word. The Bible says the earth, all of creation has been suffering under the curse of the darkness, yearning to return to the Blessed state for which they have been created. A man placed all creation under the curse. Jesus came to restore that same creation back under the Blessing. Creation is eagerly awaiting for God's people to imitate their Father and begin speak the word (*light*) to redeem the earth. *"For the earnest expectation of the creature waiteth for the manifestations of the sons of God* (Romans 8:19)." Just like God gave Adam the names of the animals, He will also give us the words to speak to calm the storm and cause the earth to cease its quaking. This is the power that God has given to His sons and daughters that walk upon the earth. This is righteous dominion.

Now is the time to exercise that dominion by speaking what our Father speaks. We will do what we see our Father do, thereby creating what He desires in this earth. *"We having the same spirit of faith, according as it is written, I believed, and therefore have I spoken; we also believe, and therefore speak* (II Corinthians 4:13)." Even in a world where the media is narrating the report of the evil one, God's people must speak *light* to come forth out of the darkness that is being reported day and night. It's as the prophet of old said, *"For, behold, the darkness shall cover the earth, and gross darkness the people: but the LORD shall arise upon thee, and his glory shall be seen upon thee* (Isaiah 60:2)." The spirit of the Antichrist is increasing in the earth, spewing evil against God and His word, but it is not his time. It is time for God's glory to manifest upon His people. Many may become offended, betraying and hating one another (Matthew 24:9), but we will obey the *light* of God's word. We don't fight evil with evil. We overcome evil with good (Romans 12:21). *"But I say unto you, Love your enemies, bless them that curse you, do good to them that hate you, and pray for them which despitefully use you, and persecute you; That ye may be the children of your Father which is in heaven: for he maketh his sun to rise on the evil and on the good, and sendeth rain on the just and on the unjust* (Matthew 5:43-44)." Evil may increase before Jesus returns, but we will plant the Heavens with love and peace. This is a different kind of warfare the world has not known.

You cannot defeat darkness with more darkness. Only *light* can take out darkness, and love is our greatest weapon. God is love (I John 4:17). Love confuses and disarms the enemy. It's the only weapon he cannot defeat because the devil does not understand love. How can you create a military strategy against God, who is Love? It's not possible. Therefore as people of faith, we take back the darkness with obedience to our Father, walking in love and speaking words of life, words that are the *light* of men. Then as the Bible says, *"the Gentiles shall come to thy light, and kings to the brightness of thy rising. Thy people also [shall be] all righteous: they shall inherit the land for ever, the branch of my planting, the work of my hands, that I may be glorified* (Isaiah 60:3, 21)." God does some of His best work in utter darkness, when mankind has lost hope and they are forced to rely on Him alone. That is why there is no need to fear the darkness of this world. God has especially equipped His people to operate when there seems to be no way. We simply realize that one word from our Father can change anything. Things may look impossible for man, but with God, all things are possible. He is the God of all possibilities and that is exactly what He is planning to display to the world in His **"Grand Finale"** before Jesus returns!

God Called The Light DAY And The Darkness NIGHT

When the Lord began talking to me about "taking back the night," it was about uprooting the works of darkness that occur in the Night and returning the night season for His purpose. The Bible says that God called *"the light Day, and the darkness he called Night* (Genesis 1:5)."* It's interested to note that when God called forth *light*, that He did not dispel the darkness. Instead, God chose to use the darkness for His purpose in ordering the Day versus the Night. Therefore the darkness serves a greater purpose than to represent the evil that we see overtaking the Night season today. Sure, evil creeps during the Night because the devil and his people have the mistaken belief that God cannot see what happens under cover of the darkness. This reminds me of the story I've told in the past.

When my son was a toddler, he used to play this game where he would place his hands over his eyes and say, "Mommy, You can't see me." He closed his eyes, and believed that if he could not see me, then I could not see him either. The only way I could convince him otherwise, was for me to do as he did. So, I would place my hands over my eyes and say, "You can't see me." That two year old laughed hysterically at me and realized how silly I looked. It was a lesson a child learned quickly. However, there are grown ups, unbelievers and Christians alike who play this same game with God, and it's not silly, but sad. They do things in the darkness at Night, as though God is blind. They close their eyes to their own sin and act like God can't see. Really? *"He that planted the ear, shall he not hear? He that formed the eye, shall he not see* (Psalm 94:9)?"* The Bible says that God knows our thoughts before we speak (Psalm 139:4). He knows the deep, darkest thoughts of our hearts (Jeremiah 17:9-10). Surely, if God sees the darkest reaches of our beings, He has no problem seeing our human bodies cowering in evil places at Night. After all, *"the secret things belong unto the Lord our God* (Deuteronomy 29:29)."*

In the end, God will judge us for what we have done in this life, every secret thing, both good and evil (Ecclesiastes 12:14). God utilizes all things for His purpose (Revelation 4:11), including that part of darkness that we call Night. It was in 1997, that the Lord first told me that **"The Night hours belongs to Me."** He ordered me on a twenty-one day fast and taught me many things, during the Night seasons. I would study the word during the Day, and at Night the Lord would give me the deeper meanings and lessons all Night long. I called it "Holy Ghost Boot Camp." I will never forget that experience. I would barely lay my head on the pillow, when the Holy Spirit would begin teaching me things about the realm of the spirit. He also taught me to keep a bedside journal for any revelations that would come during my sleep. At first, this was difficult because I wanted to respond to Night revelations by getting up, opening up my Bible and studying. It became so exhausting that I had to learn to write what I heard, and go back to sleep. In the morning I would pray and let the Holy Spirit teach me about that revelation.

It was also during the Night that the Lord would take me up to Heaven. I wasn't going to visit and spectate. I went to research the Books in Heaven, to bring back information that was needed in these last days. Only once did the Lord prevent me from coming back with information about end time events. He actually shut my body down. I was dead. He said that **"it was not time"** for certain things to be revealed. It was also not time for me to remain in Heaven. My earthly assignment had not been completed. The Lord erased it all from my mind and buried that information in my spirit. He said that when the time would come to release the revelation, the Holy Spirit would bring it back to my remembrance. Revelation from God has a specific time (season) in which it must be released. Any sooner, and it would not be received. The minds and hearts of the people would not be able to hear it. Any later, and it would not be of any use in the purpose of God. Did not God say, He was **"The Director Of It All?"** With God, **"timing is everything."** We already mentioned how God has a season for every purpose under Heaven. Even the record of my Heavenly visitations were just released, twenty-five years later. Why so late? I don't release anything until God says to do so. The very first time I went to Heaven, God demonstrated why He implemented seasons, times and signs in the earth. *"God showed me the beginning and the end. I witnessed the times and seasons of earth, laid out before God like movie frames on a digital computer screen. This was the entire work of the Father, His Son Jesus, and that of the Holy Ghost in the earth, all captured within those few frames. It was all completed before the foundation of the world. The scenes were set and the players were chosen, events were prepared before time, all for the glory and purpose of God* (Revelation 4:11)."[1]

It was within this context that the Lord showed me what He had planned for the earth. Each person and event was specifically chosen for their particular season. It was the cycle of Day and Night accumulating over years that accounted for the seasons of man on earth (Genesis 1:14). They also represent the *"signs"* for events coming upon the earth. Even in nature, we know the signs of the changing seasons from Fall to Winter, and from Winter to Spring. We know and understand the signs of changes in the weather and atmosphere. God keeps covenant with both the Day and the Night. *"While the earth remaineth, seedtime and harvest, and cold and heat, and summer and winter, and day and night shall not cease* (Genesis 8:22)."

As it is in the natural, so it is in the realm of the spirit. If God will keep covenant with the Day and Night to bring forth its season, then how much more would our Heavenly Father keep His covenant with His Children to bring forth our promises in our appointed season? *"Thus saith the LORD; If ye can break my covenant of the day, and my covenant of the night, and that there should not be day and night in their season; [Then] may also my covenant be broken with David my servant, that he should not have a son to reign upon his throne; and with the Levites the priests, my ministers* (Jeremiah 33:20-21)." Beloved, God loves us so very much, you have to believe that. No matter how dark this earth looks, God's plan for your life is very good. We must always strive to see the good, and we will find Him. God is good.

---

1   Matthews, Paula. "Times, Space, Seasons, And God's Purpose." *I Sought God And Met Him Face To Face*. Atlanta: Spirit & Life Publications[SM], 2019. 57. Print.

While in Heaven, I saw the beginning and the end of time as we will come to know it on earth. It was such a small span of time compared to the vastness of space in the universe. *"God pointed out the beginning of time. He pointed out the end of time. Then He showed where we were now on earth. It was such a small sliver from the end of time. It shook me up. There I saw it, the end of the world as we know it. The finality of it all. Here is what the Father shared with me. He has declared that this is His appointed season, a kairos moment in time and space when His will must be done."*[2] The key in all of this is that God had reserved this Day as the season in which **His will must be done** if Jesus is to return. The enemy will continue to blaspheme God and abuse His creation. The Lord is taking it all back. He has need of the Night season to complete His will before Jesus returns.

The Bible says, *"The day is thine, the night also is thine* (Psalm 74:16)." We are in a season in which God is taking all of creation back to His original plan. He is restoring our Night. It is our gift from God, where He gives His beloved sleep (Psalm 127:2) knowing that our Father has our provision and protection covered. The Night is also a time of instruction. The Lord gives us counsel in the Night (Psalm 16:7). The prophet wrote about Jesus waking up with the *"tongue of the learned* (Isaiah 50:4)." He spent the Night being instructed on who He was in the Father. The Night is also a time spiritual refueling and empowering in the Holy Ghost. Jesus would often go to the mount to pray all Night, and come down performing miracles. The Night is also the time in which God solves mysteries and gives us solutions for the issues of our day. These often come as visions and dreams in the Night. The Bible also says the Lord even gives us *"songs in the night* (Job 35:10)." Clearly, God uses the Night for the benefit of His people, which is why the enemy seeks to disrupt the Night time hours with evil and terror. The Night has become full of witchcraft and all manner of evil, but that was not God's original intent. God speaks to His people through dreams in the Night. Jacob dreamed and saw a ladder on the earth whose top reached to heaven. He saw angels ascending and descending on the ladder (Genesis 28:12).

---

2 Matthews, Paula. "Times, Space, Seasons, And God's Purpose." *I Sought God And Met Him Face To Face*. Atlanta: Spirit & Life Publications[SM], 2019. 61. Print.

Joseph had dreams from God revealing his destiny. His brothers envied Joseph and sought to kill him because of those dreams (Genesis 37:5, 9, 18-20). In Gibeon, God appeared to Solomon in a dream by Night saying, *"Ask what I shall give thee* (I Kings 3:5)." God also spoke to Daniel in Night visions (Daniel 2:19, 7:2, 7, 13). In the New Testament, God spoke through many of His people, including the Apostle Paul who had visions in the Night (Acts 16:9; 18:9-10; 23:11).

I recall one of the most powerful *visions* the Lord gave me. This *vision* lasted all Night long and left me exhausted the next Day. The vision repeated three Nights in a row. Days later, it manifested during the Day. The Lord was teaching how to minister to those in *gross darkness*. The *vision* was the same every time. Jesus and I would be standing under a huge tree on a hillside. In front of us was a line of people standing in single file. As far as the eye could see, there were people standing in this line. The line seemed endless. Who were they? Jesus never said. They had come to be set free from demonic strongholds. Each person would step up to me and Jesus would tell me what to speak and the person would be set free. Then the next person would step up to me, and again Jesus would tell me what to speak and another person would be set free. Here is the thing, these people seemed to be full of demons. Once the person would step forward, those demons would manifest as if to intimidate me. I didn't even flinch. Jesus was teaching how to minister to those whom the Church has long feared. That is why we were not in the building of a church. We were outside on a hill. This series of *visions* established a method that Jesus has used throughout my ministry. At Night, He would give me the word to speak, whether it was for teaching, preaching or ministering to His people. I would speak healing or cast out demons at Night. The person would walk free during the Day. The Lord taught me to minister at Night while I slept.

The Bible records some of Almighty God's greatest acts of deliverance that happened at Night, under the cover of darkness. God sent plague of death against Egypt at Night (Exodus 12:29-30). Moses led the people to pass through the Red Sea at Night (Exodus 14:21-31). Joshua led the people to a mighty victory at Gibeon (Joshua 10:7-

14). They marched upon them all Night. When morning came, Joshua commanded the sun and moon to stand still until they avenged themselves upon the enemy. Apostle Peter was rescued from prison by angels at Night (Acts 12:5-17). Paul and Silas were bound in prison. At midnight they prayed and sang praises to God and a great earthquake shook all the prisoners loose (Acts 16:25-30). When God's people pray, they will be rescued with a mighty hand, even at Night.

We know what the Bible says about God being *light*, but the Bible also talks about how God shrouds Himself in the darkness. *"Clouds and darkness are round about him: righteousness and judgment are the habitation of his throne* (Psalm 97:2)." God appeared to Moses and the Children of Israel *"in thick darkness* (Exodus 19:16, 20:2)." *"These words the LORD spake unto all your assembly in the mount out of the midst of the fire, of the cloud, and of the thick darkness, with a great voice: and he added no more. And he wrote them in two tables of stone, and delivered them unto me* (Deuteronomy 5:22)." This is a taste of how God uses both the *light* and the darkness, the Day and the Night for His purpose. On the human side, we operate by Day and Night on various levels as well. The literal interpretation of the Day and the Night represents chronological time, by which we record the hours and minutes. Also, the Day and the Night are used to figuratively describe the works of men. The Night is associated with spiritual slumber, sin, ignorance, ungodliness, and immorality. These are also known as the *"works of darkness* (Romans 13:12)." The Night has become the time in which people do evil, while others are sleeping, thinking that God, and no one else is watching.

The Day is associated with things done during the daylight hours, when everyone, including God, is watching. Prophetically, the "Day" represents the works of Christ, *"the Light of the world* (John 9:5)." As the Bible said about Jesus, *"The people which sat in darkness saw great light; and to them which sat in the region and shadow of death light is sprung up* (Matthew 4:16)." Before Christ, there was only darkness in the earth, much like it was before creation. Not only was the earth *"dark and void,"* so were the people in Jesus' day. Isaiah prophesied such time in which *"darkness shall cover the earth, and gross darkness the people* (Isaiah 60:2)." Jeremiah echoed the same in his day saying, *"For my people [is] foolish, they have not known me; they [are] sottish children, and they have none understanding: they [are] wise to do evil, but to do good they have no knowledge. I beheld the earth, and, lo, [it was] without form, and void; and the heavens, and they [had] no light* (Jeremiah 4:23-24)." Even in our world, with all that Jesus has done to restore humanity back to God, mankind is still dark in their thoughts and void of understanding anything about God and His purpose for their lives. We, the people of God are the world's only *light*. He showed it to me in a powerful *vision*.

It was a dark *vision*. This same *vision* appeared to me more than once. It was an eerie *vision* that demonstrated how dark our world had become. In this *vision, it was the darkest of nights. The night sky was blacker than black. There was no moon, no stars. There was nothing that defined the night sky from the atmosphere around me. I could see nothing, not even a light in a building. There was only complete darkness. I heard people's voices, but I could see no one, not even the whites of their eyes, not even my hand in front of my face. There was a thick heaviness lingering in the atmosphere. It was almost suffocating. It was the deepest darkness. Life was going on as usual in the darkness, but not a figure could be seen. I saw no form of any kind, only a faint flicker of light in the far distance. Then there was another faint flicker of light even farther in the distance. Then there appeared other flickering lights in that dense darkness. These were places of refuge from the darkness. I could hear people doing business as usual. Life was carrying on in the darkness. I could not see them, but I could hear them laughing and going about their normal activities. Most people did not seem to be going to the flickering lights that were in the distance. Only those who wanted refuge sought out the light. The Lord let me see that these were lighthouses. It was so dark that I could not see them clearly, only an outline (shadow) against the darkness. They looked like towers standing above cities, houses and businesses. They look like they were on a hill, but it was actually the light casting a shadow off the tower. In my spirit I got confirmation that God's people are the only hope for those living in darkness. They are lost and dying, but few are coming to the light, yet we must be ready to receive them. We *are the children of light, called to walk in the light as our Lord is in the Light. Outside of Him, there is no hope for the lost and dying masses.* The Lord showed me this *vision* at least twice within a two-day period. The second time, it occurred during a praise and worship service. I heard the Lord say to me, **"No evil shall befall you."** I was not fearful of the *vision*, but reality set in. This is where we are as a world. This was Isaiah 60:2-3. This was gross, overwhelming darkness. The darkness I saw in that *vision* was quite disturbing, but what concerned me more was the size of those few flickering lights that were barely seen through that thick darkness. I would have thought that Christians had made a greater impact than what the Lord was showing me. I expected to see more lights with even greater, brighter illumination to light up entire cities, but that was not what God showed me. The darkness seemed to be taking over the earth completely. However, Isaiah gave us hope saying, *"but the Lord shall arise upon thee, and his glory shall be seen upon thee. And the Gentiles shall come to thy light, and kings to the brightness of thy rising."* In other words, no matter how dark it gets, the glory of the Lord is here to show people the way back to God. Therefore, it is not the darkness that prevails, it will be God and His Kingdom triumphing over the darkness of this age. God has a glorious plan for even the deepest and darkest Night.

According to the Lord, we are in **"the end of the last days."** We are at a **"kairos moment in time."** This is **"God's appointed season to reign by His glory through His people."** This is God's Day to carry-out His will before Jesus returns. Although the darkness is very thick, the only way it could get any darker would be if God took His people completely out of the earth. That day is rapidly upon us, but there is much work to be done before it comes. Besides, the Lord is coming back for a *"glorious church, not having spot, or wrinkle, or any such things: but that it should be holy and without blemish (Ephesians 5:26-27)."* The *"glorious church"* has not yet manifested in the earth. God is in the process of **"purifying"** His people in order that they may resurrect in **"pure perfection."** Then they will be able to carry the weight of God's glory in honor when the Lord appears.

Again, the eeriness of the *vision* was not only because of the density of the darkness. My heart also stirred hearing the voices and yet seeing no one. There was no way to find those who were distressed and in harm. If they did not come to the light, they could not be rescued. My spirit was questioning how anyone could survive in a world like this. Without the Lord, there would be no hope of surviving the increasing darkness. In my heart, I said, "What's the use of living, if God is not with you, leading you through the darkness?" He is our only refuge. God is our fortress (Psalm 91:1), but only for those who trust and abide in Him. Still, it was disappointing, even sad to know that many people did not desire to go to the *light*. It was as Jesus said, *"And this is the condemnation, that light is come into the world, and men loved darkness rather than light because their deeds were evil* (John 3:19)." Evil people are already condemned to go to hell, but that was never God's plan for us. Hell was created for the devil and his angels (Matthew 25:41). I do believe that my sadness was coming from the heart of the Father. How could He sit by and watch as His creation, whom He created in love, refuse His love, and chose instead to go to hell and be consumed with fire forever?

Although Hell was never God's plan, being a loving Father, He will not force His will on us. God will let us go to Hell, if that is our choice. That goes for so called Christians too. When the Lord began talking about the Night He also referred to Christians who are sleeping and participating in the darkness and hatred of our day. They are not coming to the *light*, of which they have been called. It's as though many have been **"lulled to sleep"** by the deception of the enemy. Others are willfully making allegiances with the darkness of this world. But, according to God, the Night, has become the time in which many believers have straddled the fence between salvation and the pleasures of this world, **"that time is over."** Evil is running rampant because the devil knows his time is short (Revelation 12:12). He would love to change our times and seasons and destroy all humans off the earth before God's great end time harvest. That won't happen. Our times and season are in God's hand (Acts 1:7). God alone changes times and seasons (Daniel 2:21).

Unfortunately, too many of God's people act as though they are unaware of the times and seasons in which we live. Like the ten foolish virgins who were not prepared for the arrival of the bridegroom, they too may be left behind when Jesus comes (Matthew 25:1-13). More importantly, they would have **"aborted"** their part of the mission to preach the gospel and rescue souls from the wrath to come. It's time for the God's people to know that the time of **"playing church"** is also over. *"The night is far spent, the day is at hand: let us therefore cast off the works of darkness, and let us put on the armour of light. Let us walk honestly, as in the day; not in rioting and drunkenness, not in chambering and wantonness, not in strife and envying. But put ye on the Lord Jesus Christ, and make not provision for the flesh, to [fulfil] the lusts [thereof] (Romans 13:12-14)."*

This is the end time harvest of souls. It will be the greatest harvest this world has ever seen. God needs every able-bodied believer, alert on his and her duty. He is about to awake a spiritual sleeping giant and resurrect the dry bones of an army that satan thought had been defeated. As we said, God is restoring everything, including the plan for His people, back to His original intent, and nothing or no one can stop Him. Therefore, He commanded me to write this book as a **"call to action for the army of the Lord to arise and shine and take back the darkest of nights."** We are in **"the final chapter of Earth,"** as we know it. Jesus is coming soon. His imminent return marks a **"new era, the Kingdom era."** Before He returns, the Body of Christ has much work to do. There are some Christians who are waiting for Jesus to return for the end to come, but that is not what God is saying. Our job as the Body of Christ is to *"occupy til"* His comes (Luke 19:13)." That means we have a duty to **"Advance"** the Kingdom and hold our positions until our King arrives.

Even, while writing this book, I heard the Holy Spirit shout the command to, **"Advance!"** Jesus is not going to return until all of His enemies are put under His feet. *"Then [cometh] the end, when he shall have delivered up the kingdom to God, even the Father; when he shall have put down all rule and all authority and power. For he must reign,* *till he hath put all enemies under his feet* (I Corinthians 15:24)." **"The Kingdom Reveille has sounded"** God's mighty army is arising in the earth. We are the feet of Jesus in the earth. God will subdue all His enemies under our feet. We, the Body of Christ are commissioned to offer up the Kingdom to the Father. All things must be restored back to God's covenant for mankind and the earth.

Even as I write this book, God is ever unfolding His purpose for the end times. Again, going back to the example of creation, God saw the darkness and chose to break it up by calling forth *the light*. That is exactly what the Church is commanded to do today. Darkness has increased, even to the point of appearing to dominate the entire world. The devil has seized the Night season to do his evil plans, *"while men slept* (Matthew 13:25)." All of this happened because the Church was asleep. The enemy was allowed to infiltrate the Church and lead them away from God. Now He is calling His people out of the darkness of their slumber. He is commanding them to *"cast off the works of darkness"* and put on the *"armour of light."* It's time to put on the whole armour of God and *"withstand in the evil day* (Ephesians 6:13)." It's time to **"take a stand"** against the enemy, and having done all, to stand. God wants His mighty army to stand firm on His word and take back this earth for His Kingdom.

The Bible says that it all belongs to God (Psalm 24:1). It also says that the cattle on a thousand hills, and the beasts of the forest and the wild beast of the field are His (Psalm 50:10-11). *"The silver is mine, and the gold is mine, saith the Lord of hosts* (Haggai 2:8)." God is shaking all the nations and restoring it all, to fulfill His covenant with the inhabitants of the earth. Not only will we see the greatest harvest of souls this world has ever seen, but we will also experience the greatest wealth and power transfer known to mankind. *"Therefore thy gates shall be open continually; they shall not be shut day nor night; that [men] may bring unto thee the forces of the Gentiles, and [that] their kings [may be] brought* (Isaiah 60:11)." Nothing God is doing in this era can be stopped. That is why the enemy is to actively lying and deceiving the world. It's the devil's job to play **"keep away"** with the truth of God's love and compassion for this world. If ever there was a time for believers to take stand against the darkness of this world, the time is now. The towers in the *vision* were few and far between. They were not necessarily churches, but homes, establishments and other types of facilities where believers could be found.

We are the only *light* in this dying world. We need to show the world another way, a greater, a clear path, to be the *light* through this ever increasing darkness and take back everything that devil stole from us!

> "Ye are the light of the world.
> A city that is set on an hill cannot be hid."
> Matthew 5:14

Walking Through The Shadows

When I recall that *vision* of the spiritual darkness of our world, it struck me that I saw no shadows, except from the faint flickering lights. From a distance there were no shadows at all, but the closer you got to the towers that had light, faint shadows could be seen all around them. The thing about shadows is that they can only occur where there is *light*. In fact, a shadow is caused by objects that block the *light* from a specific region. If you place your hand over a lamp, the portion of the hand that is over the *light* will cast a shadow in the far distance, although the *light* itself will have illuminated the hand in the near distance. So, the question becomes, was the *light* illuminating the hand, or was the hand blocking the *light*? I would say both.

Remember how God saw the darkness and yet He called forth the *light* to separate or break up the darkness. Once God has established the *light*, it could never be extinguished. *Light* has the eternal purpose of exposing and deposing the darkness whether it is in a room, or in the earth itself. Shadows occur where the *light* and darkness intersect, and one passes over the other in time or space. The shadows indicate the passing of one and the beginning of another. The recording of how the shadow passes, is the way that sundials tell the time of Day or Night. Shadows are very useful in defining time, but many of us have been conditioned to fear the shadows of life. David wrote the 23rd Psalm in which he talks about walking though *"the Valley of the Shadow of Death."* This psalm is often recited at funerals, probably because of the word "Death." The Psalmist was letting us know that he walked through the valley. It was not death, but a shadow of death which had created fear in the hearts of man. It's reminiscent of childhood fears. We were taught to be afraid of the shadows in the Night. Childhood imaginations were often filled with fictitious creatures coming out at Night. In the mind of a child, any shadow could become an ominous creature that was out to get them. It didn't help that back in the days when most baby boomers were young, there was a popular radio show that our parents listened to called, "The Shadow."[1] The Opening line of the show always captivated the imagination of the audience. *"Who knows what evil lurks in the hearts of men? The Shadow knows!"* I grew up listening to radio shows at Night, but that particular show conjured up images of shadows associated with mystery, death and crime.

Many of us also grew up hearing about the *"Boogeyman"* coming to get children while they slept. Even the lullabies we heard before bedtime like *Rock-a-bye Baby*,[2] were also frightening. What kind of parent puts their baby in a cradle on a tree top? How could any child sleep peacefully at the thought of a baby falling to his hurt, or even his death? This is how American's traditionally put their young children to bed at Night. Most insidious of all is the prayer many of us prayed with our parents at bedtime. It includes the words, *"If I should die before I wake, I pray the Lord my soul to take."*[3] Would you sleep peaceful after confessing the possibility of dying in your sleep? No, and neither would a child. And, saying *"Good night. Don't let the bedbugs bite?"*[4] Really? How could thought of being bitten by any bug make for a good night sleep?

What child would not have night terrors after being put to bed in such a manner? This was the case for many of us. We were indoctrinated from childhood to fear that evil could come upon us at Night. It was done in such an innocent way, with nursery rhymes. Is there any surprise that Americans have so easily adopted a heart and mind to accept evil rather than good? We were lied to back then, and many of us still believe those lies today. The Bible says to raise up a child in

---

1   "The Shadow - 56 Mp3 Downloads Available." Old Radio World - Old Time Radio MP3 Downloads, www.oldradioworld.com/shows/The_Shadow.php.
2   "Rock-a-Bye Baby." Nursery Rhymes, allnurseryrhymes.com/rock-a-bye-baby/.
3   "The God Squad: Origin of Nighttime Prayer Is Obscure." Los Angeles Times, Los Angeles Times, 6 Oct. 2012, www.latimes.com/socal/daily-pilot/tn-dpt-1006-godsquad-20121005-story.html.
4   Bologna, Caroline. "Here's Why People Say 'Don't Let The Bedbugs Bite'." HuffPost, HuffPost, 23 Jan. 2018, www.huffpost.com/entry/heres-why-people-say-dont-let-the-bedbugs-bite_n_5a5eb9e6e4b00a7f171b947c.

the fear and admonition of the Lord (Ephesians 6:4), not in the fear of evil. God's word is so full of beautiful things about peace, love, and goodness, but I didn't recall hearing much of it in childhood, not even as an adult. Then I came face to face with evil. The enemy was threatening to take my life. I learned that it was nothing more than a shadow. Death wasn't coming to take my life. It was only a threat. Death couldn't take what didn't belong to him. My life was in Christ. Whenever I was threatened with death, the Lord would show me something in a *vision*. He would show me doing something or going somewhere. In my mind, if that thing had not happened yet, then that devil could not take my life. Deep darkness surrounded me, but the Lord *"enlightened my darkness* (Psalm 18:28)." He shed *light* on my situation and showed me a way of escape. That was half of the battle. Although the Lord was enlightening my darkness, not everyone around me saw the *light*.

People around me, even Christians noticed the evil things that happened, and began calling them good. They thought evil happened because it was God's will for my life, or because I was living in sin. My desire was to obtain everything God said was good in the Bible. People around me said it was impossible. They even feared what the devil would do to me if the goodness of God was available. They spoke as though the devil were this big old "boogeyman" who could stop me from having the *"abundant life* (John 10:10)" that Jesus came to give us. We had been conditioned as children to have faith in the things that hide under the bed, or in the closet at Night. We never saw those things, and yet we had faith that they were out to get us and to do us harm. I quickly learned that God was in **"hot pursuit"** of anyone who simply had a heart to obey Him (II Chronicles 16:9). The people whom I trusted meant well, but had little knowledge of God or His heart towards us. They never emphasized that God was good and that evil was not from Him. They didn't see Him as a *"good Father* (Matthew 7:11)." They saw God as a tyrant who was eager to punish you for doing wrong. Something deep inside of me refused to believe that about God. So, I went straight to the Source. I demanded to know the truth, and God began revealing Himself to me.

God revealed who I was to Him. What He revealed was a relationship. He was my Father and I was His daughter. **"I belonged to Him."** This was a game changer for me. At the same time, I was embarrassed that I did not know about this relationship. I knew I was saved, but that was all I knew. A deeper look back at my life revealed that as a child I had a relationship with God, but somehow the hardships of life had blocked this truth from my memory. The darkness sent by the enemy was blocking what I used to know about God. The **"light of God"** was intentionally being blocked by the devil, and I fell for the deception. Thank God for the Holy Ghost. He reminded me that I use to know the loving relationship with the Father. His love is what drew me to Him. That is why I got saved in the first place. Somehow, over the years, the darkness prevail over the truth. Eventually the truth that I knew was no longer a memory. I don't even remember how it happened, but somewhere along the line, I bought the lie that God did not care about me. The Holy Ghost didn't take me back through all the evils of my life. He only reminded me of God's love for me. It was the Holy Spirit who brought it all back to the forefront my heart and mind.

No longer did I fear death, because I knew the Father's love towards me. As the Bible says, *"There is no fear in love; but perfect love casteth out fear: because fear hath torment. He that feareth is not made perfect in love* (I John 4:18)." I knew God loved me; that He would not let any evil happen to me. Yet looking back upon my life, evil did happen and God kept me through it all. Even as I am writing, deliverance is going forth. The Lord is reminding me that evil happened because, like Adam, I gave my power to another, who was disobedient to God. As a child, we must obey our parents, even bad parents, if we want to live a long life. *"Children, obey your parents in the Lord: for this is right. Honour thy father and mother; (which is the first commandment with promise;) That it may be well with thee, and thou mayest live long on the earth* (Ephesians 6:1-3)." Being a child in an abusive home was not easy, and yet I had to obey God. The saving grace was my great-grandmother. I recall her telling me that my parents had religion, but what they really needed was a personal relationship with the loving Father. She encouraged me not to just obey my parents, but to also to pray for them to truly know Jesus. I loved Granny so much. She made the stories in that Bible come to life. She often talked about how her mother talked to Jesus face to face. Her mother was known to have raised the dead back to life on several occasions. She knew Jesus. She knew God. That's what I wanted for my life, but it was difficult being in a household where religion blocked the intimate knowledge of God. I use to write letters to God about things I was going through. He would answer me in my prayers, but I could not share these things with my family. I could share with Granny until she went to Heaven during my first year of college. I was left with no one to share the goodness of God with in my family.

Then I got married to a man who claimed to be a Christian. God warned me to stay away from the man, but we had been deceived by this man. He wasn't who he said he was, and this man really hated God. For sixteen turbulent years I endured suffering, until I cried out to the Lord for help. Why did He let me go through so much suffering and do nothing? I thought He loved me and would automatically show up to save me. God said that He could not intervene without my permission. He was waiting for me to ask for His help.

Here is a key lesson I learned about God. He cannot intervene in our human circumstances without being invited. Prayer invites Him into our circumstances. As the Bible says, *"For whosoever shall call on the name of the Lord shall be saved* (Romans 10:13)." God wants us to call upon Him in prayer. *"Call unto me, and I will answer thee, and shew thee great and mighty things, which thou knowest not* (Jeremiah 33:3)." God gave us dominion over the earth and its circumstances (Genesis 1:28). He cannot just step in and take over. We have to invite Him. Sure there is death, famine, disease and all manner of evil. The world is full of darkness and evil because of Adam's curse. Jesus restored the Blessing to us, but it is not automatic. We must first receive Him by inviting Jesus into our lives. He will not violate our will nor will He violate His word. God is not evil. He does not bring evil upon us. Evil is in this world. It cannot be avoided. That is why Jesus brought salvation. It is the way of escaping the evil of this world system. He restores the *light* to bring us out of darkness. In my adult years, I had read the Bible from cover to cover, never considering just how good God truly was. My life was in the shadows. Reading the Bible did not seem to help. I would read through the Bible, not fully understanding what I was reading, until I got filled with the Holy Spirit. Then He quickened (made alive) the scriptures and began teaching me from the Bible. The **"light of God"** began to flow out of me. I had no idea that it had been deposited inside of me. The Holy Spirit knew it was there. He would take me through the Bible and say, **"Remember when I told you to do . . . ? Here is the scripture. Remember when I spoke this . . . ? Here is the scripture."**

This went on and on until I realized that by hearing the voice of the Lord and obeying what I heard, I was fulfilling scripture. The Good Shepherd (John 10:14) had been leading me all that time. He was leading me on the path of righteousness for His Name sake. I just didn't understand back then. Jesus said that His sheep knew His voice and would not follow after the voice of a stranger (John 10:5). Jesus also said, *"My sheep hear my voice, and I know them, and they follow me* (John 10:27)." If I had not been able to hear the voice of God, I'm not sure where I would be now. The Holy Spirit has been my life saver, even before I really knew who He was. He has been the One who has enlightened my darkest of days. I could not have made it without Him.

Seeing that *vision* of the darkness, my heart wondered. "How can we know how to walk through the darkness?" We cannot make it in this world without God. Listen, Jesus could not live in this world without God. How do we know? He said, *". . . Verily, verily, I say unto you, The Son can do nothing of himself, but what he seeth the Father do: for what things soever he doeth, these also doeth the Son likewise* (John 5:19)." Jesus went even further when talking about us. *"I am the vine, ye [are] the branches: . . . for without me ye can do nothing* (John 15:5)." Jesus was talking about Christians, those who believe in Him. Now consider what the Bible says about the unbelievers in the world. The Apostle Paul describes them as being those who are, *"without Christ, being aliens from the commonwealth of Israel, and strangers from the covenants of promise, having no hope, and without God in the world* (Ephesians 2:12)." This makes it quite plain that without Jesus, there is no hope for the world. Without Him we can do nothing that is worthy of our Father's approval. Therefore they remain in the Valley of the Shadow of Death. When death and destruction comes. It is no longer a shadow for those without Christ. They have no *light* in the darkness. They have no Shepherd to lead them out. They remain with the workers of iniquity, falling deeper into the abyss and further away from God.

Darkness is a comfortable place for those who love misery and all manner of evil. It becomes like living in a cave, surrounded by your own cocoon of wickedness, never even desiring to see the *"light."* Most people think of beautiful butterflies coming out of a cocoon, but there are also other creatures who cocoon as well. Spiders and blood-sucking leeches have cocoons too. Consider that.

Not everyone will come to the *light* as Jesus said. They love doing evil. They are cursed in the world. Some chase after the things of this world. They chase after anyone and anything that would give them what they consider an advantage in life, but they won't go after God. Then there are the naysayers who are avoid of hope. Period. They see only the lack and misery. Nothing you can say or do will relieve them because they love their doomed state of living. This book is not for those who love evil whether they be in the Church or in the world. This is for those who want to live the Blessed life that God designed for mankind before the foundation of the world.

I know what it is like being surrounded by spiders, leeches and naysayers. It's a "downer" for sure. In the Church, some would say that we have to suffer through the evil until we die and go to Heaven. They believe that our only reward and inheritance is in Heaven. There was a time where I just accepted what these elders told me. It left me questioning how to live in this evil world. It didn't make sense that Jesus went about healing and delivering in His day, and it was not available in our day. It didn't make sense to me that Jesus and the apostles did miracles in their day and we had none in ours. There was a void in my understanding of the purpose of God for my life. My life was in the shadows. As a Christian, was I supposed to sit idle and watch as evil grew more evil and more people suffered and died on their way to hell? This bothered me. It didn't seem like the God I read about in the Bible who said, *"For I know the thoughts that I think toward you, saith the LORD, thoughts of peace, and not of evil, to give you an expected end* (Jeremiah 29:11)." Where was the peace God had towards us? Why wasn't evil backing down? No one around me had knowledge of the truth, so I went on a journey to question God directly. At the time I didn't know any scripture that said the Lord would *light* my path as I searched for answers in the darkness. I needed hard answers that only God could give me. Christians were walking in fear, hoping one day to find reprieve in Heaven; as if this earth is our punishment. Not so! Earth is the habitation of God, created for His kids. This was what the Father taught me.

This earth is the devil's punishment. He was kicked out of Heaven and exiled to this earth (Luke 10:18). He is beneath us. God did not create the devil in His image and likeness. Satan is a fallen angel. That devil wants our position, but he is not our equal by any means. He wants to be like man in this earth. Since that is not possible, the devil's only recourse is to influence mankind and make them rebel against God. That devil does not care what happens to us. He will use mankind and then lead them straight to their death and an eternity in hell. He envies mankind. The devil understands that the sons of God are the rightful heirs to this earth. He would like to destroy us all!

This earth is our inheritance (Psalm 2:8). We have to stand in faith and fight against the devil for what is rightfully ours. The treasures hidden in darkness belong to us (Isaiah 45:3). There is no "boogeyman" hiding in those dark places. Treasure is stashed in those dark, secret places. That treasure belongs to God and His heirs. The reason so many of God's people have never received their inheritance is because of fear of the devil. Back in the day, I wasn't even convinced that the devil was real. Boy, was I deceived! In my deception, a door opened for evil to come into my life, taking me further away from the good things of God. At some point, I believed that my education and career experience would nullify the powers of whatever evil was in the world. I know for sure that our human wisdom and powers are limited. Human intellect is no match for the supernatural power of darkness. You cannot shadow box the devil. Demons won't flee because we have an advanced college education. In fact, demons are attracted to our pride in accomplishments. As smart as I am, I could not overcome a devil who had survived thousands of years of deceiving the whole world.

That devil had another advantage over me. He had witnessed the mighty moves of God throughout history. The devil knows the truth about God and His word. He was not ignorant. I was the ignorant one; ignorant of satan's devices (II Corinthians 2:11). Sure, I had read stories in the Bible, but I thought them mere tales and folklore, even Christian myths. How could this have happened to me? I believed what the world told me about God and about the Bible. I didn't believe what I read. I believed what people told me. After all, they were adults. They had wisdom, so I thought. They had survived life. They had been where I was in life, and of course they had more knowledge and experience. I was wrong. It is not about age, or experience. It is the Spirit of God operating through us that makes us wise (Job 32:8-9). They lacked the spirit and the wisdom that came only from God.

Many people around me had never heard the truth of God. Like me, they read the Bible, but lacked the wisdom of how to use the Word of God. Not because we didn't believe God's word to be true. We thought His word impossible to achieve. We were trying to fulfill God's word on our own, without Him. This was life in the shadows. God never intended for us to walk this life alone. That is why Jesus left us the Holy Ghost. As the Psalmist said, *"The Lord is my shepherd. I shall not want."* In this world, we stumble in meeting our needs, but if the Lord leads us by His Spirit, the outcome would be sure. That is why the Psalmist said that the Lord leads us to *"green pastures"* and *"still waters."* He restores our souls. Provision, peace, healing and deliverance for our souls, all provided through the leading of the Good Shepherd. He also leads us by His Spirit in the paths of righteousness because of our enemies. The Lord makes our way straight before us (Psalm 5:8). We don't have to stay in the shadows. Jesus leads us through the Valley of the Shadow of Death. Therefore we fear no evil. That includes being fearful of wicked people and wicked circumstances, even war, famines and pestilences (viruses) that will happen in the evil day. The Lord leads us past our fears to an even greater thing. The ultimate goal of the Holy Ghost is to lead us to our inheritance in God's Kingdom which is set in the midst of enemy territory. He sets a table for us in the presence of our enemies. To feast at the *Lord's table*, we must be led into enemy territory.

Now, I know there are Christians who would say that "The communion table is the Lord's table. It's not the same as the table in Psalm 23." Really? Read it again. *"Thou preparest a table before me in the presence of mine enemies: thou anointest my head with oil, my cup runneth over* (Psalm 23:5)." Who prepared the table for us? We didn't do it. The Lord did. By virtue of who prepared it, this is the Lord's table, though it contains more than the wine and bread that represents our Jesus' death. This particular table contains our inheritance; everything that the Lord has prepared for us since before the foundation of the world (Matthew 25:34).

This book is not necessarily about our inheritance, but one must understand that our fight of faith in this life is about receiving everything Jesus lived, died and resurrected to give to us. The table set before our enemy represents the *"completed works of Christ"* on our behalf. The devil does not want believers to receive their earthly inheritances. So he distracts us with fear, lack, and sickness in the shadows. He knows that if the world would see the goodness of God, they would follow Him. The Bible says that Jesus received many wonderful things for us. In Heaven, the angels and elders sing about Jesus, *"the Lamb that was slain to receive power, and riches, and wisdom, and strength, and honour, and glory, and blessing* (Revelation 5:11-12)." At the table we will find, power, riches, wisdom, strength, honor, glory and blessing, among other things. These are just the beginnings of the *"unsearchable riches of Christ."* The Lord's table is a mystery, not placed for us in Heaven. We have no enemies in Heaven. Our enemies are here on earth, in the Valley of the Shadow of Death.

The Lord's table is not placed in a pleasant place where there are only holy angels singing beautiful songs to God. No! He prepared His Table on earth, in the midst of evil and turmoil, and pestilence and disease. It's in plain sight, for the whole world to see God's reward for the man [or woman] whom the King delights to honor (Esther 6:6-9).

God wants all of mankind restored so that they can receive the inheritance that has been reserved for them since before the foundation of the world. Once we are reconciled back to our Father, our minds must be renewed to our upgraded status in God's family (Romans 12:2). We cannot receive from God with a mind that is conformed to the ways of the world. People in the world may see death and lack, but God's people have the Mind of Christ (the Holy Spirit). They see as their Heavenly Father sees. They speak as their Father speaks. They are imitators of the God who saw darkness, but He spoke *"light"* and *light* appeared. He called those things that be not as though they were (Romans 4:17). God spoke His desire and not what He witnessed in this earth. He spoke the solution, not the problem.

Herein lies a lesson. If we want a different result in life, we must speak another word over our life. Our words are seeds that we sow with our mouths. Whatever we speak, will come to pass as a harvest in our lives. Therefore if we want what God has, then we must speak what God is speaking, and not what the world is speaking. That is the purpose of *light,* to bring a solution from obscurity; to show a way, where there seems to be no way. This is what is meant to be a *light* in the darkness. When the world is speaking famine, pestilence (virus) and death, if you don't want these things in your life, don't put their words in your mouth.

God's people are ordained to speak life and life will spring forth in obedience to the spoken word. This is how Jesus lived on the earth. Jesus was the *Light* of the world. Like those towers of light I saw in the *vision*, we come to Jesus that we might have life (John 5:40). He came to give us life, and life more abundantly (John 10:10). His words that He spoke. They are *"spirit"* and and they are *"life* (John 6:63)."
Those who live by Jesus' words will see life in abundance. The world

may be in the curse, but those who obey the word will be walking in the abundance. This is a witness of *light* in the midst of darkness. Men who desire to escape the darkness will come to the *light* to receive God's abundant life. They will see that the Lord has prepared a table for us and has given us a cup, full of Blessing that is running over with the goodness of the Lord. The Lord leads us through the darkness not just for our safety. The Lord also leads us to our inheritance (wealthy place) in Him. The Lord displays our table as an invitation to the world to come and experience the Blessing of the Lord that makes one rich without sorrow (Proverbs 10:22). He fills our cup to overflow, as we push back the enemy to free others.

Jesus sacrificed for us, therefore we ought to sacrifice for our families, our communities, cities, states and nations. We partake of the cup in persecution, suffering and hatred, for the benefit of others. Jesus set the example. *"Who for the joy that was set before him endured the cross, despising the shame, and is set down at the right hand of the throne of God* (Hebrews 12:2)." Jesus prayed in the Garden of Gethsemane before the crucifixion. *"O my Father, if it be possible, let this cup pass from me, nevertheless, not, as I will, but as thou wilt* (Matthew 27:39, 42, 44)." Jesus prayed three times saying the same words. Finally, He took the cup and sacrificed His will to the Father. The disciples who were with Him fell asleep, but Jesus demonstrated how to sacrifice our lives for others. This is also our cup as believers who follows Jesus. We all have a cross to bear. Jesus said, *"If any man will come after me, let him deny himself, and take up his cross daily, and follow me* (Luke 9:23)." We follow Him out of shadows into the *light*.

For years, darkness shadowed my life because I was ignorant about what my salvation afforded me. At the time, I did not recognize that this was the deception that devil used on Eve in the garden saying, *"Yea, hath God saith . . .* (Genesis 3:1)?" Unfortunately, I did not know what God had said about me, the believer. That would come later, so would the knowledge that this was the same devil that tempted Jesus in the wilderness saying, *"If thou be the son of God . . .* (Luke 4:3, 9)."* Satan questioned Jesus about His identity as a son of God. I didn't know my identity in Christ. Then the Holy Spirit revealed the truth and it was all over. The devil was mad. He thought I would be deceived forever. Not so! I had a hunger and thirst for truth, a truth that could only come from God. One revelation from Heaven changed my perspective and turned my life from the curse to the Blessing. God would give me a *vision* or dream that would be just enough to hang my faith on. That devil wanted me dead, but God showed me something different and I refused to fear. My desire was for what God had for my life. It was not His plan me to die, but to live and to declare the works of the Lord (Psalm 118:17). I saw death for what it really was, only a shadow. It's a threat that hangs over us, but we don't have to accept it, if we are a believer in Jesus Christ. He took death for us, but we have to remain connected to Him if we want to see life. Jesus said, *"I am the vine, ye are the branches* (John 15:5)." How does a branch wither and die? Once disconnected from the tree, a branch cannot sustain life for very long before it dies. Neither can we sustain life for long, being disconnected from Jesus. Death will come through sickness, disease, through loss of sight and mobility. These are all symptoms of death operating in the life of a person who is disconnected from the Vine.

Psalm 23 is a powerful reminder that this world in like walking through the Valley of the Shadow of Death. Evil and death are always with us because of the fallen state of humanity. The good news is that God protects those of us who will let Him *shepherd* our lives. When I earnestly sought His Face, the Lord led me to His Divine plan for my life. Since that day, I have never looked back. I continue to follow Jesus every step of the way, even in the shadow of our **"Night season."** The Night is almost over and Jesus is returning soon. The shadow of death will no longer remain, yet we will stand as the *light* in the gross darkness of this age.

When I look at my nation, which God loves, I see a people who have little or no love for that which is good in the sight of God. This is evidenced in the world around us, but most pronounced in the Church of Jesus Christ. I heard the Lord say that Americans were under a **"strong delusion."** God was not talking only about unbelievers. He blamed this **"thirst for unrighteousness,"** on those calling themselves Christians. The Bible says that *"because they received not the love of the truth, that they might be saved, . . . God shall send them strong delusion, that they should believe a lie: that they might be damned who believed not the truth, but had pleasure in unrighteousness* (II Thessalonians 2:10-11)." People who don't want truth, stay in the shadows. They walk in the darkness of the Night seasons and enjoy it. They don't want to change. My story was different. I didn't know there was a darkness or Night season in the spiritual sense of the word. I had no revelatory insight as to how it related to my life. In fact, this book was a work in progress that began in my personal journey to hear the voice God while in utter darkness. It's one thing to hear God and watch Him move in an anointed church service. It's yet another, to see and hear God when one is surrounded by darkness. Although God did mighty miracles in my life with dreams and visions, the enemy and his minions showed up even more. Even witches began chasing after me. It's the supernatural that attracts them. I cannot begin to count the death threats I still get every time I write a book. The anointing on my life stirs up the devil. Truth angers the devil and his demons. We saw how Jesus dealt with demonic manifestations.

I recall one story about Jesus being in the synagogue where there was a man with *"an unclean* [evil] *spirit* (Luke 4:33-38)." The devil in the man spoke to Jesus saying, *"Let us alone, what have we to do with thee, thou Jesus of Nazareth? Art thou come to destroy us? I know thee who thou art; the Holy One of God."* The devils knew the true identity of Jesus, even though people did not. I had similar manifestations. Demons would manifest every where I went. They seemed to come through the walls of buildings just to yell, scream or laugh at me. My presence irritated them. Some were even amused, as if to laugh at me, knowing that very few other people could actually see them. I was the *light* shining in the darkness and the devil could do nothing about it. As John said, *". . . the light shineth in the darkness and the darkness comprehended it not . . .* (John 1:7)." Jesus was the *Light* of the world, and His own people did not receive Him. This was my experience. As God's *light* was upon me, my people didn't receive me either. They were irritated by the *light*. I never had to say a word. My very presence caused demons to manifest in their lives. People kept saying that it was me; that I was carrying the demons. I could hear the voice of God very clearly, but what I was seeing was puzzling. I just could not understand why there were so many demons around me. It never occurred to me to ask God. I just assumed that since no one spoke about them, no one could see them. Maybe it was just my imagination, but time would reveal the truth. The closer I drew to God, the more I saw what He saw. The demons were still there, but I also saw the angels and the beauty of Heaven. I saw Jesus. It was wonderful! I saw the beauty of my God. I saw His protection through the angels. I saw His approval of my obedience and confirmation of my salvation. I was hungry for more. God fed me more and it caused my *light* to shine even brighter. Many people were drawn to the *light* of God that rested upon my life, but not all had good intentions. It was like what happens when a kid gets a new pair of white sneakers. Some people are so envious that all they want to do is step on those new shoes and make them dirty. Others are ready to hijack those shoes right off your feet. This was what it was like for me walking in the *light* of God's anointing.

The Night is for the Lord, but in reality, that devil never sleeps. He is constantly plotting and scheming against the people of God during the Night season. For the believer, the Night is for sleeping, for resting in the presence of the Lord. Our bodies sleep, but our spirits are connected to our Heavenly Father. Our spirits never sleep. The Bible also gives us reassurance that our God is always on His job. *"He will not suffer thy foot to be moved: he that keepeth thee will not slumber. Behold, he that keepeth Israel shall neither slumber nor sleep* (Psalm 121:3-4)." God will always preserve the way of His saints, but the wicked (those who turn away from God to do their own thing) will be left in the darkness without hope. The ways of man will not prevail.

Even now, the Lord has declared that **"the time of man's wisdom has ended."** Neither shall darkness prevail in the earth. It is time for God's people to ignore the shadows in the Night, and put their hands to the plough and work the works of God. The shadows cannot stop us if we are following our Father. God is unstoppable. It is vain to stay up late worrying about the evil one. It's a waste of time to fight with the low level devils. It's time to hold our peace and let the Lord fight the battle. Let me give you an example of what that looks like. Jesus told his disciples to take out their ship and go to the other side of the lake. A storm arose while Jesus was asleep in the hinder part of the ship (Mark 4:38-41). The disciples were so fearful that they thought they were going to die. They frantically woke up Jesus saying, *"Master, carest thou not that we perish?"* In other words, they said, "Jesus, we are going to die and all you can do is sleep?" Jesus got up and spoke to the storm and told the sea "Peace be still." Then He chastised the disciples for having no faith. If Jesus is in your ship, and He said you were going to the other side, what could possibly stop you?

Years ago, the Lord sent me on a mission in somewhat of a scary place, far from my home. I ended up staying with some people who had a demon possessed guest. I don't believe that anyone knew this person had demons. They just knew the person had issues. Well, that Night, the demons causing this person's issues decided to attack me during my sleep. There is nothing more disturbing than having a demon possessed person stand over the bed where you are sleeping, and they are praying in devil tongues.

That Night, I was tired and wanted to get some sleep. I simply turned my back on the devil and said, "Lord, I'm going to sleep, I will leave this battle to you." I don't recall speaking in tongues. I fell asleep and my spirit fought the battle from the inside. My sleep was sweet and I arose refreshed the next morning. Unfortunately, the demon possessed person went into cardiac arrest and was taken away in an ambulance. That devil tried to distract me with an attack, but I would have none of it. This was a shadow lurking in the Night. It held no danger to me, only danger to the one who chose to let her demons attack me. Hey, if Jesus could fall asleep during a raging storm, why can't I?

TAKING DOMINION OVER THE NIGHT
Treading Over All Enemy Powers

Believers have been given authority over all the power of the enemy. The spirits are subject to us (Luke 10:20), yet the Lord had me write this book to exhort Christians to stand firm in their authority. We talk a great game, but if the enemy is overtaking the Night seasons, the watchmen are not on their posts. Where are they? God says that **"many are sleeping on the job."**

What's amazing is that I've heard pulpit ministers talk about how the devil is fearful of them, the moment they get up out of bed. That's a bit presumptuous. This is no statement of that person's spiritual power over the devil. God calls it **"idle talk."** The enemy is relentless and we need to be vigilant. The Bible says that the devil walks around like a *"roaring lion seeking whom he may devour* (I Peter 5:8)." Satan walks around like a roaring lion, but he is not a lion at all. He is a defeated foe exiled to the earth. He is a lowly creeping snake over whom God gave us dominion. The Bible also says that the enemy creeps in while men are sleeping (Matthew 13:25). That devil is not intimidated because we get out of bed. He sets snares and curses against God's people all during the Night.

The spiritual battle rages at Night. That is why we pray during the Night watches. We must **"set the atmosphere"** at Night so that we can rest and continue working the ministry for another Day. This is especially true of prophetic ministers who are sensitive to the Holy Spirit. We can often be found battling in tongues even while asleep. The body is conditioned to rest while the spirit does the fighting. Sometimes it is a simple fight that requires nothing more than breaking out in a praise in the middle of the Night, or speaking a prophetic word that comes up out of one's spirit. So, to hear someone talking about the devil being scared when they get up, leads me to believe that they have never been in a *real* battle with the devil. Or, perhaps they have never fully submitted to God to qualify for a *real* battle with the enemy. Believe me, when you totally yield to the will of the Father, God will put you in *the heat* of the battle. This is to train you how to remain faithful while **"under fire."** There are battles we step into because of disobedience. Then there are the battles God thrusts us into because of obedience. If God leads you into battle, then the intensity of your spiritual attack indicates the anointing and power destined for your ministry. This will be a fight of faith to make you stronger. It's a battle where you come face to face with the devil and win. It requires that you submit to God, otherwise it is impossible to win. Take a look at the ministry of Jesus.

In the previous chapter we mentioned that demons manifested everywhere Jesus went, and not necessarily at Night. The demons would manifest because they knew who Jesus was, even if the disciples did not. The demons would manifest even in the temple. There was the time that the religious leaders led him out of the church to throw Jesus off a cliff (Luke 4:28-30). Then, it was Caiaphas the High Priest who advised the Jews to have Jesus executed (John 18:14). Do you think that any of those people were afraid of the Son of God when His feet hit the ground? No! That devil doesn't care! The Holy Spirit led Jesus into the wilderness *"to be tempted by the devil* (Matthew 4:1)." Jesus fasted and prayed for forty Days and forty Nights. Do you think that devil gave Jesus the Night off to rest? No! The Bible says that *"when the devil had ended all the temptation, he departed from Him <u>for a season</u>* (Luke 4:13)." After forty Days and forty Nights that temptation was done. The devil left, but he would come again. The devil is always on his job to deceive and **"discredit"** God and His anointed (Psalm 2:1-2, 8). Our job is to obtain the inheritance that Adam lost. Therefore we tread on the enemy and keep going forward, whether in the Day, or at Night.

Whatever the enemy plots and schemes against us is just part of the program. We are the *light* going up against the darkness of the Night. The battle has been in full engagement since Jesus came to earth. Ours is a fight of faith. I will say that again. We are **"striving against the evil to manifest the goodness of God."** Since Adam sinned, evil has dominated. Jesus came and gave dominion back to God's people, yet that devil does not want to give up any ground. He will put up a fight. Expect it, but also expect to win, especially if the Lord placed you in the battle. It was the Holy Spirit who led Jesus into that wilderness to confront the devil. This was a spiritual battle that Jesus was anointed to win. The scripture says that immediately after the devil left Him, that Jesus left the wilderness and *"returned in the power of the Spirit into Galilee: and there went out a fame of him through all the region all about* (Luke 4:14)." Matthew's gospel said that *"angels came"* and ministered to Jesus (Matthew 4:11). After this temptation Jesus was empowered to preach the gospel of God's Kingdom. Sure, that devil came, but as the Jesus said before going to the cross, *". . . for the prince of this world cometh, and hath nothing in me. But that the world may know that I love the Father: and as the Father gave me commandment, even so I do . . .* (John 14:30)."

Notice how Jesus was able to overcome the evil one. Although the devil came, he found nothing in Jesus. Meaning, there was no cause for the devil to take dominion over Him. There was no evil, no deceit, nor any offense in Jesus. He was **"strictly obedient"** to the Father. Jesus also **"set the atmosphere"** to meditate on the Father's will during the Night. We mentioned Isaiah 50 in an earlier chapter, where Jesus woke in the morning with the tongue of the learned. He never bragged about the devil being in fear because He got out of bed. Jesus showed us His secret to overcoming the devil, and this was no **"idle talk."** From this passage of scriptures, we will see that Jesus was **"fierce in His faith."** Isaiah records these words of Jesus in talking about the crucifixion. *"The Lord hath opened mine ear, and I was not rebellious . . .* (Isaiah 50:5)." Jesus had an ear to hear and obey the Father, even to death on the cross.

While writing, the Lord revealed something that never had occurred to me. He showed how Jesus demonstrated **"nonviolent resistance"** against the powers of authority in this world. This was something that had been revealed to Dr. Martin Luther King, Jr., who was an ordained prophet of God to the nations. Just as Jesus was anointed to show us the Kingdom. **"Dr. King was anointed to show us the way to resist the civil authorities and the unjust laws of our day.**

Marches ordained by God will be blessed, but those instigated by the wicked ones of the world will be confounded and put to shame. These are those who use the pretense of following Dr. King's example, but they use it to divide and invoke violence among men and to control the masses." Beloved, the Holy Spirit is speaking something I had not heard before. Dr. King was following Jesus' example of nonviolent resistance. This was a demonstration of faith and power **"under fire."** In the Kingdom we don't overcome evil with evil. We overcome evil with good (Romans 12:21). This is something people in the world do not understand. Just because you have been wronged does not mean you need to avenge yourself. If you belong to God, let Him avenge you. Keep your heart and mind free of offense. Keep your hands from doing any man wrong. You want to be able to ascend to God's Holy Hill (Psalm 24) to successfully petition Him in prayer. Only those with *"clean hands, and a pure heart"* are able to do so.

God is a righteous judge. You cannot appear before Him unclean, and expect Him not to judge you. He will judge all unrighteousness, that of the accused and that of the accuser in the same judgment. This is why many Christians have authority over the devil, but they are not able to exercise that power. They are out of position with the righteous judge. They are unclean before God. They may talk the talk, but they are unable to walk the walk the Lord has set before them. They never heeded the example that Jesus left us. Jesus didn't just talk a good game, Jesus demonstrated how to submit to God first, which empowers us to stand (resisting) in the evil Day. Only then will the devil to flee (James 4:7).

One cannot command authority over evil, without being submitted to the authority of God. As the Bible says, we must be *"strong in the Lord and in the power of His might* (Ephesians 6:10)." On our own we have no power. Remember, Jesus is the Vine and we are the branches. Without Him we can do nothing (John 15:5). Mankind has no power to fight the wickedness of this world. Our enemy works as an organized team. They are legal entities of the demonic realm of darkness. No flesh and blood can win against them. We don't wrestle with flesh and blood (Ephesians 6:13), *"but against principalities, against pow-*

ers, against the rulers of the darkness of this world, against spiritual wickedness in high [places]." Though we walk in these flesh bodies, that is not where we war. The battle waged against us in the realm of the spirit. No flesh can win in that realm. That is why we need to be one, as God the Father, Son and Holy Spirit are one. We must be one with them to wage a successful warfare and win (John 17:20-23). We need *the armor of God* for protection. We need His Spirit to guide us to victory. We must be ready and dressed for battle. We must be strong in the Lord and submitted to Him. We must align ourselves with God to successfully resists these enemy powers.

The weapons of our warfare are not carnal (of human design), but are mighty through God to the pulling down of strong holds (II Corinthians 10:4-6). There are some points that must be understood, if you want to exercise your authority over the spiritual wickedness of this world. First of all, the war is spiritual. Secondly, the weapons are spiritual. Thirdly, God's weapons are designed to pull down strong holds. This is a military tactic of God's Kingdom. Strong holds are **"fortified belief systems, established by wicked schemes of men and devices of the devil; beliefs that mankind adopted because of his fallen state that separated him from his original divine nature."** In other words, any thought adopted by man under the curse, could be considered a strong hold. It could be a myth, folklore, old wives tales, or any pagan, tradition or religious belief that did not originate from Almighty God. Taking it a bit further, this would also include educational, intellectual, sociological and political ideology based upon the recollection of historical data of spiritually ignorant and sinful men.

Understand that thoughts developed under this cursed earth system are faulty. They are substitutes for the truth of God, which Adam walked in at the beginning. When Adam sinned, he was separated from the wisdom and knowledge of God, which was to provide for the physical and spiritual sustenance of man on the earth. Sin shut off the wisdom of God. Consequently, mankind had to fend for himself. He had to provide for himself. He even had to think for himself with knowledge, not from the Creator, the Source of truth and life, but from what man could gather from the world system. Sure, life experience has counted for something throughout the generations, but it was done outside of God's original purpose for mankind. It was done in the absence of God's truth. What worked in past generations will no longer work in this world. We are in the **"final season of earth."** Jesus is soon returning to set up His earthly throne. In preparation for His return, everything is being restored back to God's original purpose. God's Kingdom is taking over, superseding human efforts. As God has declared, **"the works of man has ended. It is My time ... My time of jubilance as righteousness returns to the earth."** There, you've heard it. God says it is His time; a time of restoration of righteousness in the earth. Righteousness is God's way of being and doing right. It's His way of doing things. Period. Any other way of being is considered unrighteousness. All unrighteousness is sin (I John 5:17), but there is good news. God is no respecter of persons. If anyone from any nation fears God and works righteousness, they are accepted with God (Acts 10:34-35). If God is speaking to your heart, take a moment to pause and receive salvation today.

Say this prayer:

Dear God, I repent for sinning against you and your plan for my life. I renounce satan, witchcraft, idolatry and all manner of evil. I want Jesus as my Lord. Cleanse me from my sins and all unrighteousness. Fill me with your Holy Spirit, and I will live all the rest of my life for you. In Jesus' Name I pray. Amen.

If you said that prayer, then you are a child of God. Welcome to the Family! By faith you have been delivered from the power of darkness and translated into God's Kingdom (Colossians 1:13). You have been transformed into a new creature that is subject to God (II Corinthians 5:17). You have been reconciled (restored) back to God by His Spirit. This is why Jesus came. He said, *"I am the way, the truth and the life, no man cometh to the Father, but by me* (John 14:6)." In these end of last days, everything, and everyone must be transformed to God's Spiritual Kingdom operation. Jesus came to restore mankind, but the Body of Christ is commissioned to restore mankind and the earth (and its possessions) back to God. The Bible says that the whole creation groans for the manifestation of the sons of God (Romans 8:19). When the Body of Christ walks as sons in obedience to God, they will restore not only mankind, but all of creation back to the Father. Please understand that when Adam sinned, a curse came upon all creation (Genesis 3:17-19). Earth's creation, including the ground has been yearning to be freed from Adam's curse. Jesus came to show us the way to the Father and to restore to us the wisdom and power that God had set aside for His sons and daughters before the foundation of the world.

Our job as New Testament believers is to walk in what Jesus obtained for us and deliver up the Kingdom to the Father. We remain here on earth to finish what Jesus started. That means going after the powers of darkness and subduing them, in order to restore God's divine order in the earth. God expects His people to take a stand against the darkness (the evil, ignorance and sin) of our age. Rather than tolerating evil, God expects us to speak against it. We don't always have to confront a person, but we must confront the spirits of darkness. Remember that we war against spiritual wickedness in the heavenly places. We take authority over the demonic powers that are using people as puppets.

Jesus gave us power (authority) to tread over all of the power of the enemy (the hostiles, the haters, the wicked ones). Here is a powerful definition of what it means to tread. *"To advance by setting foot upon, tread upon: to encounter successfully the greatest perils from the machinations and persecutions with which satan would fain thwart the preaching of the gospel."*[1] This definition begins by saying, "to advance." How appropriate it is that the Holy Spirit had already commanded us to **"Advance!"** This means to step forward with whatever God had commanded for us to do. Here is the thing. Everything God commands us to do is ultimately connected to the gospel. It will be either a message, or a demonstration of the gospel in action. This is precisely why the enemy fights against God's anointed. He does not want people to hear the good news about God's Kingdom.

1   "G3961 - pateō - Strong's Greek Lexicon (KJV)." Blue Letter Bible. Web. 14 Dec, 2020. <https://www.blueletterbible.org//lang/lexicon/lexicon.cfm?Strongs=G3961&t=KJV>.

The enemy rules by fear and deception. God's Kingdom rules by truth and love. These are opposites of each other. Therefore when truth about the gospel is shared, the enemy will create distractions to deflect the truth. He often uses deception to twist the truth. It may sound like truth, but it is deception, with an underlying purpose to get one to follow after satan (or after a man) instead of following after God. There is a perfect example of this in the Bible (Acts 16:16-17) where there was a girl with a spirit of divination (psychic), who according the Bible, *"brought her masters much gain by soothsaying."* This young woman followed Paul and Silas saying, *"These men are the servants of the most high God, which shew unto us the way of salvation."* What the woman said was true, however her spirit irritated Paul and he told the devil to come out of her and immediately it left. Here is how deception works. It sounds like truth. It may even be true, however if it is coming from a spirit other than from God's Spirit, it's demonic. It takes a discerning ear and the Holy Spirit to perceive such deception. It's not so much about what is being said, as it is about who is saying it and why. One must always test the spirits (I John 4:1). If a man or woman is speaking to lead you to worship God instead of man (Revelation 22:9) that is probably the one to hear. If a man or a spiritual idol is being glorified rather than God, that is the person to avoid.

We are spirit beings. No matter what we say, the spirit behind our voice identifies what is influencing us. One could be reciting the alphabets, but the discerning ear will be able to hear demons speaking. People are deceptive, often speaking lies, but even the truth they speak is a lie. The words may be true, but if the motives of one's heart is to trap you, to lure you, to entice you to follow someone or something other than God, it's a lie. Demonic spirits can be subtle, even lustfully leading you to a place where the devil believes you are vulnerable. Remember how Eve was enticed by a suggestion of the serpent (Genesis 3:6)? The woman took the bait and began to imagine it in with her heart. This is how witchcraft works. The devil is not "all knowing." God is the One who sees and knows all. The only thing the devil can do it throw out a hook and see what lures you. That is how he works. He cannot see your heart. The devil can only see your reactions to what he throws at you. God sees your heart. *"The heart is deceitful above all things and desperately wicked: who can know it? I the Lord search the heart, I try the reins, even to give every man according to his ways, and according to the fruit of his doings (Jeremiah 17:9-10)."* There are many who are unknowingly following after demonic powers. These powers hate Jesus Christ. They hate anyone who stand firm on the gospel of the Kingdom. Recently, I heard a person speak and then later their spirit showed up in my house threatening to take my life unless I bow down to serve him. To meet the person face to face, they seem harmless, even likable, but to receive anything they speak, puts you in direct opposition to God. That evil spirit comes off of them and attempts to dominate others. On the other hand, the same thing happens with those of us who have the indwelling of God's Spirit. When people encounter us, God invades their lives with healing and all of His goodness.

The Lord gave me a demonstration of how this happens. He placed me on an office job for which I was over qualified. One day, the Lord said that with me on that job, He was able to touch the nations of the world. My job exposed me to consulates from various nations. In a *vision*, the Lord showed *that as I was speaking with people about business, His Spirit would come from me and come upon them. His virtue would flow from me to heal and deliver them. A spiritual deposit was being made, and the gospel was never preached.* Then I got the confirmation. There was a delegation from Japan heading back to their nation. The spokesperson for the group said that they had been to the city many times, but something was different about the current visit. He said that because of having worked with me, *"something had been deposited"* within them that they would *"take back"* to their country. He said they would *"never forget"* that visit. To this day, I have no idea what I did other than obey God in my daily office routine.

Spirits can powerfully influence the people around us, both for, and against God. The Bible tells the story of the mad man of Gadara (Mark 5:1-20). Demons tormented the man and caused him to cut himself. Jesus didn't try to domesticate the man. He cast out the demons and the man came back to his right mind. All Jesus did was cast out the demon. The man did the rest, and Jesus sent him out like a evangelist to his home town. We don't wrestle with flesh and blood. Our enemy is spiritual. People are in bondage to devils and our job is to set them free. Some people have no clue that they have been besieged by demons. They believe that it is really them acting and speaking out. This is the deception of the enemy.

In fact, modern media portrays demonic behavior as normal and acceptable. People will even talk about their demons. Some even believe that their bodies tell them what to do. The body simply follows the spirit and the mind. The controlling gate is the mind. If the spirit and the mind is aligned with God, then the body will follow suit. If the spirit belongs to God and the mind does not follow suit, the person will vacillate between the things of God and the things of the world, not being successful in either. Sin, guilt and condemnation will keep them following after the flesh and neglecting their spirit, until they come into the knowledge of truth. *"[There is] therefore now no condemnation to them which are in Christ Jesus, who walk not after the flesh, but after the Spirit. For the law of the Spirit of life in Christ Jesus hath made me free from the law of sin and death (Romans 8:1-2)."*

Sometimes people walk in condemnation because they don't know that they have power to tread upon the enemy. Others may know, but feel helpless against the devil. That is because as flesh and blood beings we have no power against spiritual beings. That is why we need the Holy Ghost. He is our Helper. It is by the spirit that we can defeat the devil, and he knows it. But, if Christians don't know it, the devil will have a field day at their expense. I recall something that my ex-husband told me. This man was a member of the Methodist Church, but after we married, I learned that he was practicing witchcraft. I asked why he did it. He said because it worked. When I asked why he thought it worked. His answer shocked me. He said, "Nobody obeys God." Because they don't obey God, he could do all manner of curses and witchcraft against them and it would work. I have heard pastors say that you cannot cursed what God has blessed (Number 23:8). They attempt to use that scripture, but it only applies to those who are walking in obedience to God. The Bible also says, that *"the curse causeless shall not come* (Proverbs 26:2)." Curses can't just come upon a child of God. We have to give the devil cause to strike us. Disobedience is just cause for any curse. Just in case there are some who would like to test this theory about Christians, beware. When that man attempted to do witchcraft on me, it back fired. He almost lost his mind trying to find out why it wasn't working on me. Witchcraft is a work of the flesh. We can see it operating, but as true believers, we can also override what the devil is doing. We have power over all the power of the enemy. If the witches refuse to leave us alone, God will have them taken out of the earth. He will not allow a witch to live and continue messing with His people.

As believers in Jesus Christ, the Blessing is ours. It is up to us to remain under God's protection and provision. Our disobedience leaves us uncovered. God will not bless our wickedness. Jeremiah 17:5 says, *"Thus saith the LORD; Cursed [be] the man that trusteth in man, and maketh flesh his arm, and whose heart departeth from the LORD."* In other words, when we turn away from what God has told us, even to do our own thing, we empower the curse to come upon our lives. The Word of God is subtle, but true. God is holy. He has no fellowship with darkness. Period. The covenant in the Blood of Jesus cleanses us from all unrighteousness (sin), but only if we repent. If we sin, we simply confess our sins, and God is faithful and just to forgive our sins and cleanse us from all unrighteousness (I John 1:6-8). Then, we are restored into right relationship with the Father and back under the Blessing.

In America, we want God to Bless a nation that has intentionally cut off and ignored the covenant we have with Him. There is a spirit in the land that has exalted itself above God. Some would call it the human spirit or humanism. If it's not God's Spirit, then it's mostly witchcraft. All rebellion is considered witchcraft (I Samuel 15:23). Even those who pretend to be spiritual leaders can be under witchcraft. They may sound like preachers of truth, but they have a different spirit, just like the woman with the spirit of divination. It may sound right, but it's not right. It's not the right spirit. Historically, we have seen charismatic leaders both religious and political, lead people to death and destruction. The people were brainwashed under a spell of witchcraft. This is why the spirit of divination (witchcraft) is so dangerous. It is a spirit that works to lure people to follow after anything and anyone else but God. Then leads them to their demise, and finally to hell. The Bible is very strict about punishment for those who practice witchcraft, soothsaying, psychic, etc. These are all spirits that want to replace God in your life.

The ex-husband who did witchcraft hated God. He also hated those who served God. Why was he in a church? He was looking for "good Christian girl" to destroy. He admitted that was his plan for my life. He declared that he was "the only god I would ever serve." Really? Who says that, but a demon possessed witch? They are deluded into believing that they are more powerful than God. All because they don't see immediate divine punishment for their actions. There is a scripture that speaks to that. Solomon said, *"Because sentence against an evil work is not executed speedily, therefore the heart of the sons of men is fully set in them to do evil* (Ecclesiastes 8:11)." This refers to those who don't fear God. The righteous man or woman who fears God, will be quick to repent. As a child, there is nothing more terrifying than waiting to get spanked, especially if it didn't happen right away. It was delayed punishment. You knew it was coming. Why was the parent tormenting you by delaying punishment? Why the torment? We feared the wrath of the belt. A longer delay meant more severe pain and punishment. We just wanted to hurry and get it over with.

The opposite is true for those whose parents never seemed to punish them. They thought they were big and bad until something or someone bigger and badder took them down. That's God. He lets us go on in sin for a while. That is His mercy towards us, but when sin is full, the punishment will surely come. Solomon echoes the same by saying, *"though a sinner do evil an hundred times, and his [days] be prolonged, yet surely I know that it shall be well with them that fear God, which fear before him: But it shall not be well with the wicked, neither shall he prolong [his] days, [which are] as a shadow; because he feareth not before God* (Ecclesiastes 8:12-13)." There it is. The days of the wicked are *"as a shadow"* because they don't fear God. Judgment may not come right away, but it always comes. The Old Testament punishment for witchcraft is severe. *"Thou shalt not suffer a witch to live* (Exodus 22:18)." Today, anyone who gives their life to Jesus Christ can be spared this and every penalty of death. Anyone who continues to practice, after salvation and will not repent, shall have their place in the lake of fire. They won't be in Heaven (Revelation 21:8; 22:15).

Listen, it doesn't take much to be considered one who practices witchcraft. The Bible says that rebellion is witchcraft. What is rebellion? It is the willful act of disobeying God to satisfy our own needs. It's any act of controlling and manipulating (playing God over) another person's life or their property or any of their belongings. Witchcraft is akin to covetousness, when people lust and envy something that belongs to another. We have a commandment that says *"thou shalt not covet…* (Exodus 20:17)." If you are a Christian praying evil or soulish prayers to either hurt or benefit yourself or another, repent. If you are a practicing witch, repent. God wants to deliver you. Repent. Renounce satan and ask Jesus to be your Lord. You cannot continue and win. Death is the penalty for those who refuse to repent from witchcraft. As a man sows, that shall he also reap. As the Bible says, *"Be not deceived."* God will not be mocked (Galatians 6:7). You can take that to the bank.

We are talking about treading upon all the power of the enemy, and specifically we are focusing on witchcraft as being **"enemy number one"** to God's Spirit. It's satanic in nature, attempting to *"exalt"* one's throne above the Most High God (Isaiah 14:13). Some would argue that we have a human spirit; that we are free moral agents to do as we please. Sure, but our human spirits are not independent from the influence of the spirit realm. They are aligned with one of two spirits. Either we are with God, or against Him. We are either under the influence of the kingdom of darkness, or the Kingdom of *Light*. There are only two spiritual kingdoms from which mankind operates. God's Kingdom brings the Blessing, while the kingdom of darkness is under the curse. At salvation we are snatched out of the power of darkness and translated (transferred into) God's Kingdom (Colossians 1:13). It's one power or the other. There is no in between. We have to make a choice between the Kingdom that offers life and the Blessing versus that which offers death and the curse. *"I call heaven and earth to record this day against you, that I have set before you life and death, blessing and cursing: therefore choose life, that both thou and thy seed may live (Deuteronomy 30:19)."*

In God's Kingdom, we automatically qualify to walk in power as the sons of God. The authority to tread upon all the power of the enemy belongs to us, but it can only be enforced as long as we are obedient to our Father. Otherwise our power to tread is not effective. Remember that our enemy is very organized. Devils don't break rank. To tread, we must not break rank with our Father either.

Let's return to our story about Paul and Silas. We're still talking about the authority to tread upon all the power of the enemy. In this particular case, Paul being irritated by the demon in the young girl, was determined to cast that spirit out of her. He took authority over the spirit and set the woman free, but her handlers were not happy about it. Here is something to note. All the systems of this world have been built under Adam's curse. We talked about how after Adam, all of mankind's knowledge had to be gained from observing the world around him. His efforts to govern was based upon dealing with cursed men. His methods of commerce was based upon the financial corruption of wicked men.

So every one who comes out of that system has to be educated on the ways of God's Kingdom. They cannot follow God using the same tactics of the powers of darkness. It won't work. God is a holy and righteous God, who expects us to walk in His ways. You can no longer walk any way you want and get the results of God's Kingdom. In the case of the young woman with the spirit of divination, she was a tool of commerce and trade for her handlers. Obviously she made them quite a bit of money because they were so angry at Paul for terminating their source of income.

Listen. Anytime you remove someone from the cursed world economy, there will be backlash. We saw this when God sent Moses to deliver the Children of Israel out of Egyptian slavery. God's people were undergirding the economy of a pagan nation that despised them and their God. The Hebrew slaves built Egypt and caused it to be a great power in the world. In fact, it started with their ancestor Joseph who brought the world's wealth into that nation. For over four hundred years, Pharaoh abused the very ones who caused His nation to be blessed with wealth. The slaves were vital to Egypt's sustained wealth. God honored His covenant with His people and delivered them out of the hands of Pharaoh. Before they left Egypt, God recompensed them for what they had lost in finances. They spoiled (plundered) that nation of its wealth (Exodus 12:36).

We saw the same thing when Jesus cast the legion out of the demoniac. The unclean spirits asked to be sent into a herd of swine feeding in the area. Imagine a legion, which some estimate to be about six thousand demons that left the body of one man and entered into a couple of thousand swine. It's not known how long this man had this legion, but there was no relief for him until Jesus showed up. Here is something to consider. The swine could not withstand the demons. They ran down a steep hill and drowned in the sea. What had possessed one man for years, sent a herd of swine immediately to their destruction. Spirits can powerfully influence human beings, even possess them. This gives you an idea of the spiritual capacity of man. We were created to "house" the Spirit of God and His Kingdom, but in the absence of God, many have found themselves like this man, filled to spiritual capacity with demons. This was never God's plan for those created in His image and His likeness.

The best part of this story, is that the man was restored back to his right mind. It was a wonderful thing for this man, but not everyone was happy for him. The people in the town were upset at what Jesus did. Obviously this was a great financial loss to the one who owned the two thousand pigs (Mark 5:15). They wanted Jesus to leave before He caused any more losses to their economy. The same is true in the world economy today. The wealth of the world was built upon the backs of slaves, and now God is setting them all free. The devil won't be happy, but God's covenant with His people must be fulfilled, no matter what. We will tread upon all the financial power of the enemy. God will **"bust up"** their witchcraft scheme of slavery. Pharaoh must let God's people go.

Like that demoniac, many Christians are bound by the devil. They talk a good game, but in reality, they have not taken back the Night from the wicked one. Most Christians are oblivious to the darkness that stalks even at noonday because they are asleep spiritually. Many think that knowing the scriptures, or reciting the scriptures gives them power over the devil. Only the word that we meditate on and act on has power. Those who hear the word and get excited, may seem motivated, but those who do the word are committed to the word that they hear. No believer has to fear the terror by Night. If we are abiding in God's word, then no evil shall befall us and no plague will come near our dwelling (Psalm 91:10). This includes all forms of evil, even viruses and pandemics; riots and wars.

For the most part, God's people are asleep while battles are raging in our neighborhoods, cities and nations. Those controlled by the devil devise iniquity and work evil in their beds at Night (Micah 2:1). The devil does his best work against God's Kingdom, in the darkness, when God's people are sleeping (Matthew 13:25). Beloved, wake from your slumber and repent. Do not fear tens of thousands who have set themselves against us. God will break the teeth of the ungodly (Psalm 3:5-7).

God has taught me the importance of being available for His work in the Night seasons. When the Lord would wants to show me something of great importance, or that contains great detail He has me wait on Him during the Night. Most times, God would have me pray in the spirit all Night long. Jesus prayed all Night and came doing miracles the next morning (Luke 6:12). God spoke to His apostles and gave them ministry direction at Night (Acts 16:9; 18:9-10; 23:11). There are many stories about the great works of God that happened at Night. If the Lord is the same yesterday, today and forever (Hebrews 13: 8), why haven't we seen more of these things happening in our day? God's purpose for our times and seasons, has not changed. The divine purpose **is** the same. In fact, the Lord gave me a strong word about what He is doing in these end of the last days. He called it a *"Divine Reversal."*

The *"Divine Reversal"* actually began when Jesus resurrected from the grave. As the Bible says, *"For this purpose the Son of God was manifested, that he might destroy the works of the devil* (I John 3:8)." We not only have power to tread upon all the power of the enemy, but God is in the process of *reversing* every evil thing the enemy had planned for this earth. God has declared this to be the season to display His *"Grand Finale before Jesus comes."* It's a season of God's justice to make right that which has been set against His people and His covenant for the earth. There will be a spiritual *"Exodus"* from the bondage of the evil one into the freedom which is in Christ. God is promising to do something of *"Biblical proportions."* If He did it once in the Bible, He can do it again in our day.

God is willing to do the same and even more for those who trust Him to take care of impossible situations in their lives. Faith requires acting out what you believe, regardless of how it looks to others. In the end of last days, we will perform *"greater works* (John 14:6)*"* than what the Bible records. Don't be surprised. This is the end. Jesus is coming soon. Every prophesy concerning the Church has to come to pass before Jesus returns. The devil has been opposing the divine prophetic move in this earth, but no longer will it be tolerated by God. Enough is enough!

No longer will the saints of God lie down and sleep during the Night. The devil may plot, but we will take dominion over our Night time hours. It's our time of instruction from the Lord. It's time for us to *"set the atmosphere"* to meditate on who we are in Him. We have tremendous power when we have a heart to obey the unction to pray in the Night seasons. We need to make ourselves available to intercede whenever the Spirit calls upon us. It not only is to advance the Kingdom, but also to sow seeds into the lives of those whom God wants to reach. God will show Himself strong on our behalf. *"For the eyes of the LORD run to and fro throughout the whole earth, to shew himself strong in the behalf of them whose heart is perfect toward him* (II Chronicles 16:9)."

The Night time is God's season of power. It's the time God often sends His people into battle to cut off the plans of the enemy before they begin. The Night season is not the time for spiritual slumber. It is the time in which God bestows His greatest blessings upon His people. It's when the effectual prayers of the righteous avails much power (James 5:16). Prayer is key to the power in the Night seasons. We must watch and pray. This does not mean that we lay awake all Night. No! We pray and leave the results to God. We stay awake spiritually. We meditate on the word Day and Night (Joshua 1:8), not falling prey to the snares of the enemy, but letting the Lord visit us in the Night, to deliver us, to instruct us, to fill and refresh us, and to awaken our ears to hear as the learned. This is our strength. This is our power in the Night season.

Knowing Our God And His Covenant

We are talking on the subject of **"taking dominion"** over the darkness of the Night and restoring God's season of power. We've learned that Jesus gave us power (authority) to tread over all the power of the enemy. We learned that in order to exercise our authority over the devil, we must be submitted to God (James 4:7). The devil's team is very organized. They operate as one. Therefore, we must be **"one"** with God as the Father, the Son and the Holy Spirit are one (John 17:20-23). Before we can become one with God, we must know Him. The Bible says, *"But the people that do know their God shall be strong, and do exploits* (Daniel 11:32)."

Our strength comes from knowing our God. In and of ourselves, we have little strength, but in God we become strong in the Lord and in the power of His might (Ephesians 6:10). It all begins with *knowing* our God. This only comes from an intimate relationship with the Father. It's not just about going to church, or reading the Bible or praying. It's all of that and more. You can read about God, but the real power is being in His presence and letting Him reveal Himself to you. Jesus said that if we loved Him, then He and the Father would love us and *manifest* themselves to us (John 14:21). Even ministers of the gospel can find themselves so busy doing the work of the ministry that they don't spend time with God. There is a story in the Bible about Martha who was *"cumbered about much serving"* while her sister Mary was seated at the feet of Jesus (Luke 10:38-42). Martha complained to Jesus hoping He would persuade Mary to come help her serve. Here was His response. *"Martha, Martha, thou art careful and troubled about many things. But one thing is needful: and Mary hath chosen that good part which shall not be taken away from her."* Jesus said it, *"one thing is needful."* The one thing that is necessary for a prosperous life on earth is learning from the Master. Jesus said, *"The kingdom of heaven suffereth violence, and the violent take it by force."* In other words, there is great warfare in obtaining the benefits of the Kingdom. You must press in to receive what God has for you. There is no amount of human effort manner that yields your divine inheritance. It has to be taken **"*forcibly*"** by faith. It begins with hearing a word from God. And, if you want to hear something from God, you must sit with Him. Jesus said, *"Come unto me, all [ye] that labour and are heavy laden, and I will give you rest. Take my yoke upon you, and learn of me; for I am meek and lowly in heart: and ye shall find rest unto your souls. For my yoke [is] easy, and my burden is light* (Matthew 11:28-30)." Jesus said, *"Come unto me . . . and learn of me . . . and ye shall find rest . . ."* The Psalmist said, *"One thing have I desired of the LORD, that will I seek after; that I may dwell in the house of the LORD all the days of my life, to behold the beauty of the LORD, and to enquire in his temple* (Psalm 27:4)." The Father and the Son desire to make their habitation with us. They want to commune with us. That's personal and intimate.

Imagine how life would change if Jesus or the Father came to live with us. Like Martha, we may be trying to work a ministry, or build a church for the Lord. If the Lord is in our house, it is more *needful*, to be still before Him, enjoying His presence and learning from Him. Mary sat at the feet of Jesus. We have the Holy Spirit inside of us. The Lord is in "our house" for sure. He is our teacher. He brings to our remembrance what the Father says in His Word (John 14:26). We don't have to see the Father with our human eyes to get to know Him. Jesus said that if we have *seen Him*, we have seen the Father (John 14:9). Therefore, knowing God is knowing the Son. We also have the Holy Spirit, and we have the Bible (Word of God).

There is no difference between God and His Word. They carry the same power. Jesus is also the Word. The Bible says that *"In the beginning was the Word, and the Word was with God, and the Word was God* (John 1:1)." So the more we study the Bible (the Word), the more time we spend with Him in prayer, the more we will learn about both the Son and the Father. Praying is more than talking to God about what we want. It's communing with Him and letting His Spirit speak to us about what is important to Him. It's having a hunger and thirst to know Him and His will (Matthew 5:6). There are great benefits to spending time with God. The Bible records how God used mightily those with whom He had an intimate relationship. The Lord spoke to Moses *"face to face"* as a man speaks to a friend (Exodus 33:11). It was David who wrote, *"He made known his ways unto Moses, his acts unto the children of Israel* (Psalm 103:7)." In other words, God demonstrated through Moses, how He (God) administers righteousness and justice in the earth. The plagues against Egypt were the "works (wonders)" of God that were displayed before the world. *"And I will stretch out my hand, and smite Egypt with all my wonders which I will do in the midst thereof: and after that he will let you go.* (Exodus 3:20)." It is interesting to note that God chose to use His wonders to war against Egypt. He sent ten plagues against that nation when He could have just spoken the word and set the people free. Instead, the Lord chose to take His time and sent a myriad of wonders against that nation. Why did He do it this way? It was an answer to a question that Pharaoh brazenly asked Moses, when the Lord sent him saying *"Let My people go."* Pharaoh responded *"Who [is] the LORD, that I should obey his voice to let Israel go? I know not the LORD, neither will I let Israel go* (Exodus 5:2)."

God sent His wonders against that nation so **that they would come to know Him by reputation**. God could have sent His Word and freed His people. But so that Pharaoh and all of Egypt would come to know Him, Almighty God stretched forth His Hand with wonders against that nation. God's people had been enslaved In Egypt for over four hundred years. They knew Him, by memory of the generations that went before them. Egypt had many gods. They knew nothing about the God of the Hebrews. Since Pharaoh asked, *"Who is the Lord . . . ?"* God was obligated to answer him. It was not a simple introduction. It was a demonstration of His power through signs and wonders, that brought terror to that nation, and freedom to the Children of Israel. God wants to be known. He is all about having a relationship with His covenant people. From the foundation of the world, God had relationship in mind for His human creation. He placed His Spirit within those who are born-again for the purpose of communion with us. When Adam sinned, the communication link between God and man was broken. Jesus came are reconciled mankind back to God. The Holy Spirit is our **"uplink"** to the Father. He searches the deep things of God and shows them to those who diligently seek Him. He is our Helper and Guide in this life. The Prophet David wrote, *"Blessed is the man whom thou choosest, and causest to approach unto thee, that he may dwell in thy courts: we shall be satisfied with the goodness of thy house, even of thy holy temple* (Psalm 65:4)." Isaiah says it yet another way, *"For I will pour water upon him that is thirsty, and floods upon the dry ground: I will pour my spirit upon thy seed, and my blessing upon thine offspring* (Isaiah 44:3)." God Blesses those who of their own free will come to Him hungering and thirsting to know Him more. The Bible says that those who come to God must believe that He exists, and that He is the rewarder of those who diligently seek Him (Hebrews 11:6).

Under the old covenant people knew that God existed because like Pharaoh, they witnessed His wonders. There are many stories in the Bible in which God made Himself known to man by various signs and wonders, even through His prophets. When Jesus came along preaching the Kingdom and doing mighty works, the first thing people would have assumed is that He was a great prophet of God. The Jews in particular were accustomed to seeing signs and wonders from those whom God sent. What threw many of the Jews for a loop was the fact that Jesus came announcing Himself as the Messiah, King of the Jews. Although He spoke God's words and demonstrated mighty works, the temple leaders refused to believe that someone among them could actually be the Son of God.

Rather than believe the evidence before them, they picked up stones to kill Him. *"Jesus answered them, Many good works have I shewed you from my Father; for which of those works do ye stone me? The Jews answered him, saying, For a good work we stone thee not; but for blasphemy; and because that thou, being a man, makest thyself God* (John 10:32-33)." Why would anyone get upset because he or she calls themselves the son or daughter of God? It elevates a human being to the level of a deity. People have an issue with those who say or demonstrate that they are of God. In the American culture, we have those we call idols in Hollywood, in entertainment and industry. People can them gods. Some call them icons, but in the eyes of God, if we elevate mankind and worship them, they are idols (gods). Icons are considered gods in their field of endeavor. These types of gods are acceptable in the world system. If you want to see the heathens rage, just call yourself the son or daughter of the Most High God. People will call you crazy. This what Jesus did and they accused Him of blasphemy.

Beloved, when you start moving in the things of God with signs and wonders, be prepared to be mocked. "You think you're God." No, I am the son [or daughter] of God doing the will of my Heavenly Father. "If God is your Father, who is your mother?" Jesus answered that for you. *"And he answered them, saying, Who is my mother, or my brethren? And he looked round about on them which sat about him, and said, Behold my mother and my brethren! For whosoever shall do the will of God, the same is my brother, and my sister, and mother* (Mark 3:33-35)." Here is one last saying of those who are envious God's grace on your life. "Who are you, the Holy Spirit?" "You're so heavenly minded that you are no earthly good." These are common mockings from those who will be intimidated by your good works. They say these things because they don't know God or His son. Obey God and keep on stepping.

The world needs to see Jesus in our day. They need to recognize that God really did send Jesus into the world, and that He is the same, yesterday, today and forever. God wants to be known through His people. Jesus came to show us God. He came as the glory of the Father, full of grace and truth (John 1:14). The disciples said to Jesus, *"Shew us the Father."* Jesus responded, *"He that hath seen Me hath seen the Father* (John 14:8-9)." Did Jesus physically look like God? How could this be? God is a Spirit (John 4:24). Jesus was flesh and blood. Jesus was not talking about physical appearance. Jesus said,

"Believe Me that I am in the Father, and the Father in me?" Jesus had often said that if they didn't believe Him, to believe *"the works"* that He did (John 10:38). Then words He spoke were not His, but the Father's. When He spoke the Father's words, it was the Father who did the work (John 14:10). God was known by the works that were performed by His Son Jesus. Amazingly enough, Jesus makes a bold statement about believers. *"Verily, verily, I say unto you, He that believeth on me, and the works that I do shall he do also; and greater works than these shall he do; because I go unto My Father* (John 14:12)." This is a revelation for many a Christian, that we are to do *"greater works"* than Jesus did. He commissioned believers to go into all the world and preach the gospel of the Kingdom, *"not with enticing words of man's wisdom, but in demonstration of the Spirit and of power* (I Corinthians 2:4)." These are the words of the Apostle Paul. He knew that if the gospel is to be preached, it has to be demonstrated by the Holy Spirit and power. Remember that God makes Himself known by doing wonders in the earth. If we are going in His Name, signs and wonders should follow us as well. This is proof that God is with us, that He sent us. This is not only for the apostles and prophets and anointed preachers. God intended for signs and wonders to *"follow them that believe* (Mark 16:17)." Do you believe? Then signs and wonders should follow you as well.

Jesus promised that if we went forth preaching, He [the Lord] would work with us, confirming the word with signs following. Does this sound familiar? It should. Recall what Jesus said happened when He spoke the Father's word [preach]. The Father would do the work [signs and wonders]. That was Jesus. Then as we go out and speak His words, the Lord works with us (doing the work), producing signs that follow the word. It is the same thing that Jesus said happened to Him. See how we can do the *"greater works?"* All we have to do is follow the same steps that Jesus walked in the earth. Jesus revealed to us a pattern of how God's wonders are displayed in this earth. It begins with the word from God. When Jesus spoke God's words it provoked the Father to do the work in producing wonders.

This is how we begin to look like our Father God. Jesus said something that is also true. *"I speak that which I have seen with my Father: and ye do that which ye have seen with your father* (John 8:38)." If God is our Father, then the works of our Father will be seen in us. We saw this same pattern with Moses. When he went to Pharaoh speaking God's words, he was made *"a god to Pharaoh* (Exodus 7:1)." Moses was not God, but when he went under the instruction of God, speaking the words of God, in essence he was representing God. Therefore, when Pharaoh saw Moses, he was seeing God. Even after Jesus' crucifixion, it was noted of His apostles, *"that they had been with Jesus* (Acts 4:13)." Their boldness of speech. The miracles, signs and wonders they performed, gave evidence that God was with them as He was with Jesus. We are still taking about taking dominion over the Night by knowing our God, and *doing exploits* (wonders). This is the end of the last days. These are the days in which Jesus is expecting the Church to do the *"greater works."*

Here is a recent prophecy from God concerning the *"greater works."* **"The works of man has ended. It is My time," says God, "to perform the greater works through my faithful servants in the earth." "For it is time for the Greater Glory to be revealed. As I have said, the glory of the latter shall be greater than the former. For all things are new, more powerful than before because time has come for the return of My Son, and there is much work to be done before He comes. Therefore I have turned up the heat upon my enemies and my foes, it will cause the glory to become even greater upon My Faithful Ones."**

Before we can perform the *"greater works,"* we must know the Father. It begins with His word (the Bible), and the word that He speaks by His Spirit to our hearts. Therefore, we must know *His Voice*. Jesus said, *"My sheep hear my voice, and I know them, and they follow me* (John 10:27)." When we think of sheep, we think of Jesus being the *"Good Shepherd."* He leads us by His voice. This is where many Christians are left behind. One must be led to do the *"greater works."* The Holy Spirit is your guide. Hearing the voice of the Lord is more than hearing a sound. It's relationship. There are still people in the Church who don't know that Jesus is real. They believe what the Bible says about Him, but they have no evidence in their lives that He is real. Some don't even know if they are saved. Many have joined churches, never having received Jesus as Lord. They don't qualify. The *"greater works"* are reserved for believers in the faith, not just people in the Church. Jesus said, *"He that believeth on me, the works that I do shall he do also; and greater [works] than these shall he do* (John 14:12)."

The Church of Jesus Christ in America is filled with unbelievers. They go to church, hear a message, and go home with no understanding of who Jesus was or why He did what He did. Many people are attracted to the idea of Jesus, but they don't care to know Him on a personal level. For some, today as well as back in His day, Jesus was more of a **"sideshow attraction."** They didn't understand His words. Many still don't. They come to see the show. For that reason, Jesus taught in parables to make a difference between those who desired to know the things of God, versus those who did not.

Not everyone who came to Jesus wanted to know about the Kingdom. They came for the entertainment value of seeing miracles, signs and wonders. Jesus was no fool. He knew what was in the hearts of men (John 2:23-25). Others came for the food. Believe it or not, when word got around that Jesus was feeding the multitudes, people came running for the free food. Here is how Jesus reacted. *"Jesus answered them and said, Verily, verily, I say unto you, Ye seek me, not because ye saw the miracles, but because ye did eat of the loaves, and were filled. Labour not for the meat which perisheth, but for that meat which endureth unto everlasting life, which the Son of man shall give unto you: for him hath God the Father sealed* (John 6:26-27)."

Jesus was not impressed with the crowds that showed up to hear Him teach. He taught in parables to the masses, and explained the mysteries to His disciples. *"It is given unto you to know the mysteries of the Kingdom of heaven, but to them it is not given . . . because they seeing see not; and hearing they hear not neither do they understand .*

. . for this people's heart is waxed gross and their ears are dull of hearing, and their eyes they have closed; lest at any time they should see with their eyes and hear with their ears, and should understand with their heart, and should be converted, and I should heal them (Matthew 13:11-15)." The masses heard His voice, but they had no understanding because the word had fallen on ears that were dull of hearing. They could receive no *light*. They could not see what Jesus was offering. Their eyes were blinded. Therefore, the word was unfruitful in their lives. However for those whose eyes and ears were open to receive the word, would bring forth fruit. They would have more in abundance (Matthew 25:29). Therefore, Jesus said to His disciples, *"But blessed are your eyes, for they see: and your ears, for they hear. For verily I say unto you, that many prophets and righteous men have desired to see those things which ye see, and have not seen them; and to hear those things which ye hear, and have not heard them* (Matthew 13:11-13)." In short, knowing the Father and the Son, requires that one be open to see, hear and obey the word that is being spoken to them. This is the person who receives the word with a *"honest and good heart* (Luke 8:15)," and produces fruit (evidence).

There are many people calling themselves Christians, yet not all are the sheep that hear the voice of the Good Shepherd. They are not following Jesus. These are people who go to church, but they do not hear nor do they know the voice of the Master. Yet, Jesus has not given up on them. He is still reaching out to them. *"Behold, I stand at the door, and knock: if any man hear my voice, and open the door, I will come in to him, and will sup with him, and he with me* (Revelation 3:20)." For Jesus, it is a matter of "Do we love Him?" Jesus said that if we love Him, then we will keep His commandments. Then there is a promise that when we keep the commandments, that both the Father and the Son would love us and manifest themselves to us. That manifestation was not only to *"sup"* with us, but to abide with us (John 14:21, 23-24). God not only wants us to know His Voice, but to know His Ways, His word and His Holy Spirit. God wants to be with us in every possible way. That is why Jesus came as *"Emmanuel, which being interpreted is, God with us* (Matthew 1:23)."

God sent Jesus so that the Father could spend time with us like He did with Adam in the garden. We may not be able to walk with the Father in *the cool of the day* like Adam did (Genesis 3:8). But, we have the word. We can walk with God as we walk through His Word. We may not hear the audible voice of God like Adam did, but, the more we study God's word, the more familiar we become with His voice and how He speaks. The Bible reveals the thoughts and intents of the Father's heart towards us. The ministry of Jesus was essential in showing us the Father. He came revealing Almighty God as a good Father. Knowing God and His Son is the true meaning of *eternal life* (John 17:3). It is not something you get when you go to Heaven. *Eternal life* begins at salvation. It's a relationship that begins as a *light* that shines out of the darkness (II Corinthians 4:6), that grows ever brighter the more we learn about both the Father and Jesus. We enter into covenant with them, and become partakers of what they have agreed upon for the sake of the Kingdom. We become one as the Father and Son are one.

To perform the *"greater works,"* one must become intimately acquainted with the Holy Spirit, who is third person of the godhead [The Father, Son, Holy Ghost]. The Holy Spirit is the **"Executor of the Covenant."** His assignment it to reveal the things that belong to the Father (John 16:14-15). He also reveals our individual callings and inheritances which the Father prepared for each of us before the foundation of the world. Not only does the Holy Spirit reveal our inheritance, but He also empowers us to receive that which God says belongs to us. It is the Holy Spirit who imparts to us wisdom and revelation of both the Father and the Son.

The Apostle Paul prayed for believers entering into this covenant with the Father and the Son. *"Wherefore I also, . . . Cease not to give thanks for you, making mention of you in my prayers; That the God of our Lord Jesus Christ, the Father of glory, may give unto you the spirit of wisdom and revelation in the knowledge of him: The eyes of your understanding being enlightened; that ye may know what is the hope of his calling, and what the riches of the glory of his inheritance in the saints, And what [is] the exceeding greatness of his power to us-ward who believe, according to the working of his mighty power, Which he wrought in Christ, when he raised him from the dead, and set [him] at his own right hand in the heavenly [places], Far above all principality, and power, and might, and dominion, and every name that is named, not only in this world, but also in that which is to come* (Ephesians 1:15-21)."

Paul prayed that we receive *"the spirit of wisdom and revelation"* in the knowledge of God. This is spiritual knowledge that comes through relationship. Again, the more we desire to understand the ways of the Father, the more abundantly He will give to us. This is revelation knowledge. *"Flesh and blood"* does not reveal this to us, but it comes from the Father which is in Heaven (Matthew 16:17). Paul also prayed that *the eyes of our understanding* are enlightened. We talked about how so much of God's Kingdom is shrouded in a mystery. Our eyes must be opened. Our darkness must be enlightened. It is the Lord who illuminates our darkness. He lights the candle of our understanding (Psalm 18:28). In this prayer, Paul specifically prays that our eyes be opened to *"know what is the hope of His calling."* To know God intimately, means knowing His calling and purpose for our lives.

We said in an earlier chapter that God has *a time and season for every person under heaven*. The Holy Spirit opens our eyes to God's wisdom *according to His eternal purpose* which He purposed for us in Christ Jesus (Ephesians 3:11). Knowing our purpose, means knowing how we fit into the plan of God for this earth. With that purpose comes an inheritance and great power to carry out that which the Father has destined for our lives. It is a purpose that cannot be obtained without God's power working through us. It has to be a partnership. *"Now unto him that is able to do exceeding abundantly above all that we ask or think, according to the power that worketh in us* (Ephesians 3:20)."* God never calls us to do what we can do by our own power. He wants the glory for doing impossible things through our lives. These are the *"exploits"* that are available to those who know their God. We, who know our God, also know that is not us, but the Father working through us to do His will and pleasure. *"For we are his workmanship, created in Christ Jesus unto good works, which God hath before ordained that we should walk in them* (Ephesians 2:10)." We are *laborers together with Him* (I Corinthians 3:9)" for the purpose of carrying out God's will. It's God's word and His power working through His people to carryout His will in the earth.

In these last days, we will see the *"exceeding greatness of His power,"* that has been designated for those who believe. This is the same power that raised Jesus from the dead and sat Him at the right hand of the Father. With that same power has God raised us up to be *seated together* with Christ (Ephesians 2:6). *"As He is, so are we in this world* (I John 4:17)." We are His Body, the Body of Christ. We are His hands and feet working the will of the Father in the earth. The power that God gave Jesus has been given to us to complete our divine destinies. The glory that God gave Jesus has also been given to us (John 17:22).

Jesus glorified the Father. Now is our time to do the same. Jesus said, *"Father, glorify thy name."* Then replied the Father from Heaven, *"I have both glorified it, and will glorify it again* (John 12:28)."

God's **"Grand Finale"** has begun. His people will *glorify His Name once again*. We will go forth in the Name of Jesus taking dominion over the darkness of this world. We will bring forth the restoration of God's Kingdom in this earth! We decree and declare that His is the Kingdom, His Will be done. For the power and glory belongs to Almighty God now and forever! Amen.

Discerning Truth From Lies

This is *"the end of the last days"* before Jesus returns. In His own words, Jesus gave us the signs of His return, *"For false Christs and false prophets shall rise, and shall shew signs and wonders, to seduce, if it were possible, even the elect* (Mark 13:22)." We are witnessing that deception in the nations of the world. God said that America was under a *"strong delusion."* A delusion is an accepted belief that is commonly held, despite evidence to the contrary. Delusion is an obvious form of *"self deception."* We know the truth, but refuse to recognize it as truth (Romans 1:21). That's what God said is happening in America, His covenant nation. Because we have no love for the truth, God is letting us walk in delusion until we come to the end of ourselves. The Lord says that **"Destruction is heading your way America, but not all will be destroyed."** Surely destruction shall come, but it will not be the portion of *those who know* their God. For there is a remnant of believers in the land.

Indeed, deception is great in the world. We have witnessed many *false prophets* speaking lies. Although there are false prophets in the Church, they are not all voices of those calling themselves Christian. That *"lying spirit"* is everywhere in the world. **"When you throw away the truth, all that remains is the lie."** There are two choices when it comes to *"veracity."* God's standard of truth is more than facts. It's about the integrity and trustworthiness of the source. For example, according to God, one false prophet is *"the American news media."* The Lord gave me a clear understanding in a *vision*. *"In this vision, I saw this larger than life arena that had a huge stage. On the stage was a performance that had captured the attention of the entire world. The Lord pulled back the scene and I saw a puppet master hovering over the stage, pulling the strings of every performer. Then I heard the Lord say, **'The performance is being narrated by the news media.'"**[1]

---

1   Matthews, Paula. "Are You Watching The Puppets On The Stage?" *GRACE For Living Magazine Fall 2020 Digital Edition*, 15 Oct 2020.11. www.graceforlivingmagazine.com.

What was the reason for such a magnificent performance? God said it was a ***"distraction."*** Why the distraction? What was it that the devil did not want the world to see? There was something more powerful was going on outside of that arena. The glory of the Lord was moving in the earth. God was moving money and power into the hands of those whom He could trust. Healing was flowing mightily to God's people. The devil could not stop what God was doing, so he decided to create a distraction to blind the minds of those destined to receive from the goodness of God. As I am speaking, there a continuous Blessing flowing out of Heaven, but you have to have eyes to see and ears to hear what God is doing in the earth. This is not the time to be distracted by the performance on the world stage. It's time to be alert and attentive to the Spirit of God, especially in the Night season, when He reveals His secrets.

The Lord taught me the importance of taking back the Night for His Kingdom. That devil knows how important it is too. That is why he devil does much of his evil while men are sleeping. I'm not just talking about sleeping in one's bed. The devil likes to catch us sleeping on the job as well, in a spiritual stupor. Praise God, who is our Keeper. He neither slumbers nor sleeps (Psalm 121:4). God is a good Father who is always watching over us with loving kindness. He will wake you in the middle of your sleep and give you a word to intercede. That is when I heard the word about America's ***"strong delusion."*** Those words woke me out of a sound sleep and my spirit began praying. This is my witness that the Night season belongs to the Lord. He gave us the Night for a period of rest and restoration in Him. We have a *covenant of peace* (Ezekiel 34:25). We can go to sleep in peace because it is the Lord that causes us to dwell in safety (Psalm 4:8). God gives His beloved sleep (Psalm 127:2). The enemy has attempted to rob us of this peace, especially in the Night season.

As covenant people, we hold the ultimate authority over the Night season through our Father. God established the seasons with His word (Genesis 1:5, 14). He called the Day and the Night by name. They were established to **"delineate the times and seasons for God's pur-**

pose" that would be fulfilled in the earth. Jesus said to His disciples, *"It is not for you to know the times or the seasons, which the Father hath put in his own power. But ye shall receive power, after that the Holy Ghost is come upon you: and ye shall be witnesses unto me both in Jerusalem, and in all Judaea, and in Samaria, and unto the uttermost part of the earth* (Acts 1:8)." God's power is in knowing our times and seasons in this earth. Our power comes from receiving the Holy Spirit and allowing Him to lead us in witnessing the resurrection of Jesus Christ. When God desires to change our times and seasons, He will speak through His prophets. God will do nothing in the earth without first revealing it prophetically to His people.

What God reveals, is truth that He wants us to put in our mouths and decree over the earth. What is revealed will be spoken and initiated in this earth through the Blessing. Remember that God Blessed mankind not only to be fruitful and multiply righteousness in this earth, but He also wanted us to *"replenish and subdue"* the earth. That means anything deviating from God's design, can be corrected by decree. Likewise, when we declare that we are in **"end of the last days,"** or that we are in a **"kairos moment in time,"** or when the Lord commands us to **"take back the Night,"** these are prophetic words from the Father declaring our times and seasons. They are also commands God expect us to follow.

We don't make those declarations on our own. These are the thoughts, purposes and intents of God. Whatever we hear from Him, we declare it in the earth. *"Thou shalt also decree a thing, and it shall be established unto thee: and the light shall shine upon thy ways* (Job 22:28)." Therefore, anything that deviates from what God has declared, disturbs our peace. It violates our covenant, and must be brought back in submission to the Word of God. When the enemy speaks deception, God's people are supposed to challenge every word with the truth. God's word is truth (John 17:17). Understand that we may be Americans, or Asians, Africans by native birth in this world. When we become born-again, our citizenship is in Heaven. Every believe can honestly decree what Jesus told Pilate before He was crucified, *"My Kingdom is not of this world* (John 18:36)." We are in this world as *"ambassadors for Christ* (II Corinthians 5:20)." We are not to conform to the thoughts, ways, nor culture of this world. We don't distinguish ourselves by race, gender or nation. We are all one in Christ. People look on the outside. Is it a male or female, Black or White? No! God sees no difference. He is no respecter of persons. He looks at the heart. Unity begins in the heart, with a love for what God loves. But, when you have a nation whose political leaders backbite one another, yet speak like they want unity, they are false prophets. Their words may say one thing, but their actions prove otherwise. The devil is deceiving the whole world (Revelation 12:9) into believing he wants to unify the people. That's his job, but we have the *"Spirit of Truth"* residing within us. He will lead us into all truth.

As believers, we are commanded to cast down all opinions and arguments that exalt themselves against God. We use God's word to pull down *"strongholds"* of the mind (II Corinthians 10:4-5). A *stronghold* is a type of reasoning (rational or not) that fortifies one's opinion. In the Kingdom a *stronghold* is an opinion or thought that defies God and His word. For example, Jesus said, *"I am the way, the truth, and the life: no man cometh unto the Father, but by me* (John 14:6)." In America, there are many people who are offended by this saying of Jesus. They refuse to believe that there is only one way to God. Did they test the saying to see if it were true? Probably not. Now, there are some Muslim converts who found out that Jesus spoke the truth. These were people who earnestly cried out to God, and Jesus responded. *"Then shall ye call upon me, and ye shall go and pray unto me, and I will hearken unto you. And ye shall seek me, and find [me], when ye shall search for me with all your heart* (Jeremiah 29:12-13)."

Only the truth of God can discern and tear down a strong hold. A person must be willing to seek the truth of God. This means seeking truth about ourselves, about others and about situations in our lives. The reason satan and his demons took over the Night, was because God's people did not discern the truth about the purpose for the Night. They didn't have *"eyes to see"* that there was no "boogeyman" at Night. Sure, the devil is busy at Night, but so is our God. Sure, he sends all manner of deception and witchcraft during the Night, to infiltrate your mind with wicked dreams and visions. That devil is an impostor. Call him out at Night for what he really is; a lying devil. Once you know what God says in His word about *a thing*, then you can fight back, even in your sleep with *"It is written* (Matthew 4:4)." That is how Jesus fought the devil in the wilderness. We will talk more about waging a warfare against the devil, in the next chapter. For now we want to focus on our discernment; having *"eyes to see, and ears to hear"* truth. There are even strongholds concerning truth itself. Some people believe that truth is relative to one's perspective in life. Wrong! That defines an opinion or one's experience, but that does not make it truth for all the world to live by. Some will even refer to "my truth," or "your truth." **Truth is absolute, it comes from God.**

The world at large is in a battle for "truth and justice," both of which come from God and His word. Even our courts have difficulty discerning truth when administering justice. It all comes down to the witness of men and the evidence they produce, and men lie. They deceive and scheme one another in order to win. Where is the justice? If you want to know truth and justice, the place to start is with God. He is the revealer of truth (Deuteronomy 29:29) and He loves justice (Psalm 37:28). In a bit, we will go into detail about how God's discernment can heal and deliver a people from an evil deception. In these last days, deception will become even greater as men attempt to hold on to their power over the masses. Don't just link up with anyone who sounds good. Don't even criticize or mock someone you don't understand. God is doing a **"new thing"** in this **"new era."** You must discern whom you are fighting before stepping into a fight. This kind of discernment comes from God. Only God can reveal the truth about His creation. He knows what's in us, from top to bottom, inside and out. God is the manufacturer of every human, spirit, soul and body. He knows the mechanics of our entire being. So, if we want to know truth about us or the truth about anything that is created upon the earth, just ask God. *"If any of you lack wisdom, let him ask of God, that giveth to all men liberally, and upbraideth not; and it shall* *be given him* (James 1:5)." In fact, the Bible says that the Word of God is more powerful than a *"two-edged sword."* It is a powerful weapon for the purpose of discerning the truth. *"For the word of God [is] quick, and powerful, and sharper than any twoedged sword, piercing even to the dividing asunder of soul and spirit, and of the joints and marrow, and [is] a discerner of the thoughts and intents of the heart* (Hebrews 4:12)." I remember the Lord telling me years ago, that His word is like a **"minesweeper."** The Word of God permeates the deepest part of our being **"detonating"** the things within us that could destroy our lives. The Bible talks about the *"washing of water by the word* (Ephesians 5:26)." The Word of God is a **"cleansing agent."** It cleans and sanctifies us. The more time we spend studying the word, the more it cleanses us. As it cleanses us, our discernment increases even more.

Then there is the *prophetic* word spoken to our spirits by the Holy Spirit. It is more powerful yet. It is powered by the Blood of Jesus, and comes straight out of Heaven. The *prophetic* word has been known to cleanse and deliver immediately on the spot. *"He sent his word, and healed them, and delivered them from their destructions* (Psalm 107:20)." We saw this in Jesus' ministry. He spoke the word only and people were made whole (Matthew 8:8). Even so, discernment is not a one time event. We are to continually *"renew"* our minds with the Word of God (Romans 12:2). That means increasing our ability to see with the eyes of God. We must be open to seeing more of what God want to prophetically reveal to our spirits. This a characteristic of one who continues on into increased levels of maturity in Christ. *"But strong meat belongeth to them that are of full age, even those who by reason of use have their senses exercised to discern both good and evil* (Hebrews 5:14)." This process of ever increasing wisdom and knowledge should continue until one is called home to glory. There are too many "baby" Christians walking around in the flesh. They have yet to be trained to walk in authority as the sons of God. The Holy Spirit is the teacher, but many refuse to be trained. Religion has convinced them that they know all they need to know about the Lord. That's not scriptural [*one thing is needful*]. What they are really saying, is that they know *all they want to know* about the Lord.

The Bible says that those who are led by the Spirit of God are the sons of God (Romans 8:14). However, the devil has deceived some into believing that the Holy Spirit is *not needful* in our day. Really? Jesus could not survive in this world without the Holy Spirit (John 5:19). He let us know that we can do nothing without Him either (John 15:4-5). Throughout this book we have emphasizing our **"divine partnership"** with God. We were created as His workmanship, and pre-ordained for a specific work (Ephesians 2:10). This is not about going to church and praying baby prayers. This is divine destiny, and yet I can name the people who said to me, "I don't need all of that."Really? What about what God needs from you?

Listen, God approached me and asked, **"Paula, are you ready to become a son?"** I had no idea what that meant, but coming from God, I knew it had to be good. So, I said yes. He said that He didn't save me for myself. I was happy to be free, but to the Father, this was not enough. He explained that I had an assignment to fulfill, which required **"growing up"** in the things of Christ. According to the Lord, this is the issue with most of the Church. We have learned how to **"do church, but have yet to walk as sons."** God is revealing a **new breed**, a remnant of believers who **"see what others don't see and hear what others cannot hear."** They will walk and talk as the Spirit leads them. They will march into the darkness of this world, and take dominion. This **new breed** of spiritual warrior will discern truth in life's situations. They are *fed up* lies and deception. They desire to know truth. Therefore they will call upon the Name of the Lord and be saved (Romans 10:13). The Lord will answer them and they will gladly follow Him. As Jesus said, *"And other sheep I have, which are not of this fold: them also I must bring, and they shall hear my voice; and there shall be one fold, and one shepherd (John 10:16)."*

God desires to give us His wisdom (spiritual insight) to recognize truth from deception. He would that we are able to discern the will of the Father, from that which the evil one has sent forth. For example, as I am writing this book, the world is experiencing what some call a "pandemic." A virus has entered earth's space. The heads of nations and health organizations have been experimenting with the mental health and welfare of the world's population. The world media has been blanketing the masses with fearful statistics about the virus and death. God is not moved by the virus. It is not stopping His purpose in the least bit. Consequently, what Almighty God is speaking from Heaven is in direct opposition to what world leaders would have you believe. The people are starting to suspect that science does not have a solution. They are doing what they know, but **"they don't know enough."** Here is where discernment from God comes into play.

While the media and health professionals are reporting the numbers of people infected and dead, God is calling the virus **"dead."** Anyone who is listening to God will hear a different message than the media is reporting. That's because the Holy Spirit is the *"Spirit of Truth."* It may be a fact that there is a virus in the earth, but God said that **"COVID is dead."** God's **"truth always changes the facts."** Let's talk truth for a moment. Jesus saw blind people. That was a fact, but when Jesus spoke the word, they were no longer blind. They could see. That's the truth. Jesus saw people who were lame since birth. That was a fact, but when Jesus ministered to them, they were able to walk. That's the truth. Shall we continue? Jesus saw many who were possessed by demons. That was a fact, but Jesus cast the demons out. The people were set free. That is the truth. This is how God's word works in the earth.

Jesus' left us with examples to follow. He did, and said, only what the Father told Him to do and say (John 5:19-20). **Jesus operated in truth that changed the facts**. He first heard a word from the Father. Jesus acted upon what He heard, and situations changed. Even concerning His own crucifixion, Jesus spoke the truth to his disciples about what would happen to Him. *"And Jesus going up to Jerusalem took the twelve disciples apart in the way, and said unto them, Behold, we go up to Jerusalem; and the Son of man shall be betrayed unto the chief priests and unto the scribes, and they shall condemn him to death, And shall deliver him to the Gentiles to mock, and to scourge, and to crucify [him]: and the third day he shall rise again* (Matthew

20:17-19)." This was the truth that Jesus spoke about His crucifixion and resurrection. When Jesus died, the disciples mourned because they did not discern the truth that He spoke when He was with them. Even when the women witnessed the resurrection, the disciples still did not believe. They thought Jesus was dead. Indeed He was. That was a fact, but Jesus told them that on the *"third day"* He would rise again. Even when Jesus appeared to them, not all believed that it was He. Nevertheless. Jesus was crucified and He died. On the third day, He resurrected from the grave, just as He had told them. This is the truth of the gospel that we preach. That if anyone confesses with their mouth the lordship of Jesus over their lives, and they believe in their heart that God raised Him from the dead, they shall be saved (Romans 10:9). Let me take a moment to extend the invitation. If God is tugging at your heart, stop right where you are. If Jesus is knocking at your door, turn to the last page of this book and read the *Salvation Prayer*. Then return to this page.

Truth must be discerned. Let's see it from a slightly different angle. In our creation example we said that God saw darkness, but He called forth *light*. The darkness was the problem. It was a fact that there was vast darkness in the earth. To make the problem go away, God simply spoke the solution. *"Light Be!" Light* responded to the voice of God and it appeared out of the darkness. It was there all along, just hidden by the darkness. The same is true today. We may see a virus in the earth. The virus is a manifestation of darkness. The solution is the truth that God has already revealed. **"COVID is dead."** We can either keep talking about the darkness and it remains, or we can speak the solution and it goes away. There is a spiritual law at play. Jesus said, that we shall have whatsoever we say (Mark 11:23). Life and death are in the power of our tongue (Proverbs 18:21). It's not what others say. It is what we say that determines our outcome in life. So it is important to discern truth before opening our mouths to speak. Solomon said that there was *nothing new under the sun* (Ecclesiastes 1:9). If that's true, then every issue *"under the sun"* has a solution that exists. It's hidden in a mystery that only God can reveal. Whatever troubles we have on earth, they are no surprise to God.

He saw it coming, and prepared a solution. The Bible says that He knows the end from the beginning (Isaiah 46:10). Of course, He's the Creator, **"the Director of it all!"** The Bible also says that *"the worlds were framed by the word of God* (Hebrews 11:3)." God is *"upholding all things"* by the word of His power (Hebrews 1:3). Although mankind has dominion over this earth, that dominion is within the framework of God's purpose and design. Mankind can speak his own words and devise his own schemes, but ultimately God's word will have its place in this earth (Psalm 33:10-11). In other words, **"What God created in the earth, no one can destroy nor remove it from the earth." "God, alone, has the true power of destruction, but He cannot violate His word."**

If God is bound by His word, then so is all of mankind. Even if wicked men cook up some master scheme to destroy every human being on the planet. If it is not within the will of God, it won't happen. Man does not have that power. God and His purposes are **"unstoppable."** The creators of this virus are men who think they are powerful because they can kill. Not so! As Jesus said, *"And fear not them which kill the body, but are not able to kill the soul: but rather fear him which is able to destroy both soul and body in hell* (Matthew 10:28)." **"God can not only kill, but also condemn your soul to an eternity in hell. That is final and eternal destruction."** I heard these words in my spirit. What we see happening in earth, is only a small part of our lives, when compared to eternity. There's more to come when you die. It's not over by a long shot. We are eternal beings who will either spend an eternity with God, or apart from Him in eternal damnation. Man has power, but only God is "all powerful." That is why He is Almighty God.

Let me make this plain. We are in a battle between Good and evil. God alone is GOOD (Mark 10:18). God created only good for us. The devil he hates the good that God has prepared for us. He comes to *"steal, kill and destroy"* the abundant life Jesus came to give us (John 10:10). That evil one cannot stop God. His only recourse is to bring threats of sickness and perversion of all kinds to turn people away from good and bombard them with evil. That is how much that devil hates human beings. It takes discernment to be able to see the distractions that block the goodness of God. Threats of death are also distractions. They cannot stop what God wants to do in our lives. We don't fear what men can do to us (Hebrews 13:6). What happens in this earth is not the end of the story. This is not the end of our lives.

What we do on earth determines where we will spend eternity. Which side will you be on? God's or the devil? Don't be fooled into believing the deception. This earth is not all that there is. The battle on the earth is spiritual. There are two fathers of spirits; One good and the other evil. One brings the Blessing, the other curse. One is Love, the other is hate. One is the Source of Life, the other comes to destroy life. The battle on earth, is for the souls men and the souls of nations. God wants to do you good. The devil wants to pervert you, steal from you and destroy every good thing God designed for you. That's his modus operandi. Therefore, concerning this so called "pandemic," it is evil. All sickness and disease, is evil. It did not come from God. The virus is a fact, yet God spoke the truth about the COVID. It's **"DEAD!"** But, here is thing. Because mankind has dominion over the earth, God has to find human beings willing to speak His solution in the earth. God has been waiting for His people to call the virus what He calls it; **"Dead."** Let me share what happened to me.

Recently, I was seated in the car outside of a market when out of nowhere, the Lord said to me, **"Didn't I tell you that COVID is dead?"** This is how God speaks to Paula. He puts me on the spot. Sure, He told me that, months after the virus had reached the United States. God said it clearly back then. **"COVID is dead."** I believed God the first time He told me. I also recall declaring this word and then letting go of it for a while. I believed that it was already done. I went about my life waiting for confirmation that the virus was over, done, **"Dead."** I also recall the Lord saying, that the virus would **"leave just as quick as it came."** A year later, and we are still dealing with the virus. What happened? God said that His people heard the truth about the virus, BUT **"the word was not mixed with faith in them that heard it** (Hebrews 4:2)." This is what God spoke to me. We heard it, but didn't take faith action. Why was God bringing COVID up now? He seemed to be a bit offended. Or maybe the Spirit was just *grieved* that His people did not discern the truth about the virus. Jesus felt that way about His disciples many times. Had we forgotten that Jesus is the Healer? He went to the cross to set us free from sickness and death. *"But he was wounded for our transgressions, he was bruised for our iniquities: the chastisement of our peace was upon him; and with his stripes we are healed* (Isaiah 53:5)." If Jesus took stripes on His body for our healing, why are Christians fearing a virus? If the Bible is true, then *"There shall no evil befall thee, neither shall any plague come nigh thy dwelling* (Psalm 91:10)." The Bible also says, *"Now the just shall live by faith: but if any man draw back, my soul shall have no pleasure in him* (Hebrews 10:38)." As people of God we are expect to walk by faith and not by sight (II Corinthians 5:7).

Without faith, it is impossible to please God (Hebrews 11:6). He is not pleased when His people go after a vaccine instead of going after the Healer who has the cure. We have a covenant promise from God. *"Behold, I will bring it health and cure, and I will cure them, and will reveal unto them the abundance of peace and truth* (Jeremiah 33:6)." Listen, I am not telling you not to get the vaccine. No! If you choose to get the vaccine, put your faith in God and not in the vaccine. Speak words of healing and faith over those affected by the virus. Take dominion over it in Jesus' Name, while doing all the law requires. Don't think that the vaccine is the cure. **"It is not,"** says God. Pray that the scientist seek God for answers. Pray that God gets the glory for what happens in this earth, concerning all things. Be mindful of God and His power and not of what men say or do. God is a jealous god.

How do you think God feels when His people yield to the opinions of experts who walk in darkness, rather than coming to the Father who is *Light*. I understand why God stopped me in my tracks questioning me. It caused me to wonder if indeed the virus had died and the **"deception"** was causing it to live longer. Remember that mankind has dominion. Our words give power to the things in the earth. If mankind keeps hearing in the news how the virus is raging, and people begin saying what the news is saying, then we, the people are keeping this virus alive with the power of our words. I also had to remember that God said, **"the performance"** on the world stage was being **"narrated by the news media."** He called them the **"false prophets"** in the world today. That means that a false narrative is continuing to give life to the **"Dead"** virus. What can God's people do? Many of them are speaking what they see and not what God is saying. They are speaking death.

To speak God's word, one has to see and hear (discern) what the Spirit of God is speaking concerning a thing. Paula has no excuse. I heard from Heaven. God shook me up. Then God made a bold declaration of His Will concerning the virus. He said, **"Before the end of the year [2021], COVID will be removed from the face of the earth."** Okay now, Paula has words she can pass on to others of like faith. We have ammunition to take out this virus supernaturally. This is the will of God. What He speaks, He will bring forth in the earth. This is how Jesus operated. He said that when He spoke the Father's words, then it was the Father that dwelled within Him that did the work (John 14:10). The same is true for every son or daughter of God. We must hear the word of the Father. Once we speak what He speaks, the Father will bring it to pass.

Immediately, I began speaking what God spoke. In fact, I asked Him, "Why wait until the end of the year? What about this month?" The Lord responded, **"this month."** Since that conversation, I just declared COVID dead and removed from the face of the earth, immediately. What's a month versus a day? God can do it in an instant. I believe that the sooner, the better. It could even be gone before this book is published. Another day, of people panicking and racing to get a vaccine is more than enough. People are trusting in a man to deliver a solution that God has already solved. There has to be a showdown between the "so called experts" and Almighty God. They are calling forth the death of people by the same virus that God is calling **"Dead."** They are promoting the virus as if it is something needful. In reality, they are training people to follow orders, even evil orders that harm and not heal. This is the spirit of the Antichrist. God is about to step into this **"spiritual hoax."** God is calling forth His Truth in this season. He wants the COVID dead and removed from the earth. So, be it, in Jesus' Name. Discernment is vital. We must be able to hear what God is speaking in every situation. Then we are able to discern truth from lies, and good from evil.

In the example of the COVID, many are calling evil "good" and good "evil." You cannot take dominion over the Night without knowing which side you are fighting. Is it good? Or, is it evil? You have to be able to discern the enemy that you are fighting, lest you be found to fighting against God and end up losing your life. To understand this more clearly, let's go back to the garden of Eden. God gave Adam one commandment. *"And the LORD God commanded the man, saying, Of every tree of the garden thou mayest freely eat: But of the tree of the knowledge of good and evil, thou shalt not eat of it: for in the day that thou eatest thereof thou shalt surely die* (Genesis 2:16-17)." It was never God's desire that mankind have knowledge of evil. Everything God gave man at creation was *"very good* (Genesis 1:31)." God, Himself is good. Everything He ever purposed and created for mankind was good. So, there was no need for mankind to know about evil. Even if they had wanted to know about evil, God would have told them all they needed to know.

God gave mankind every good thing. The only thing restricted from them was one tree from which God told man not to eat; *the tree of the knowledge of good and evil.* Why did they choose to eat from the knowledge of good and evil? It's simple The very thing that they were told not to touch, intrigued them. It got their attention and when the serpent deceived them, it was easy to lure them to their deaths. This is how the devil operates. He places something before our eyes that looks good and desirable. Then we partake of it and walk into a **"death trap."** It is always a trap of the enemy. He is not our friend. Here is another Bible truth. *"There is a way which seemeth right unto a man, but the end thereof are the ways of death* (Proverbs

14:12)." When Adam made the choice that seemed good to him, but it opened the door of death to all of mankind. That same spirit [rebellion] is ever present today. Sinful men and women have a heart to do evil. Then there are those who deliberately choose to do evil and call it "good." The Bible says, they are cursed (Isaiah 5:20). We see this type of wickedness from those in power over nations, over industries and over religious organizations. Wicked men rule in unrighteousness and they call it righteous. They persecute and demonize anyone who does not go along with their wicked ways. We're not just talking about unjust laws that promote what God has deemed as sin. We are talking about depraved wickedness that changes the truth of God into a lie (Romans 1:25). They don't care to retain God in their knowledge. They know the judgment of God and just don't care. Not only do they commit evil, but they take pleasure in others who do the same. Therefore, they are without excuse before God.

Let's go back to what God said about America being in **"strong delusion."** God said these words concerning the 2020 Presidential Election. He also graced me to be able to discern the spirits that began operating in the lives of those running for political office. In early October, I saw the glory of God rise upon the person of President Trump. He had just been diagnosed with COVID. God revealed that He was dealing with the president at the time. A week or two later the Spirit of the Lord said to me, **"A second term is granted to Him."** Immediately the Lord gave me *vision* in which I saw a crown being placed upon the head of President Trump. This was similar to what I saw the first time he was elected. God had made it clear that Donald Trump would remain the President of the United States.

Why did God give me such specific details about the election? I believe it is so that at least the **"chosen and faithful"** would know the truth and speak it into existence. Never once did God mention Joe Biden becoming president. In fact, *in a vision, the Lord showed Biden, Harris, Obama and Mrs. Clinton, and a host of others loaded on the back of a truck like prisoners. It looked like something out of a Nazi prison camps. They all had their hands cuffed behind their backs.*

There were armed guards taking them off the trucks. The first person off the truck was Joe Biden. He had a smirk on his face. The last two people remaining on the truck was Mrs. Clinton who was offended that she had been corralled like an animal and put on the truck, and finally there remained Barack Obama who was petrified, refusing to get off of the truck. These people were not going to prison. In my spirit, I sensed that they were going before a firing squad. Even while writing, God gave me another *vision* in which an angel was sent to Mr. Obama announcing that the Court of Heaven's judgment against him, was to appear before a **"firing squad."** Was this a literal firing squad? Only God knows for sure.

There are many demons on assignment to take down the nation and to turn America away from its divine destiny. They are working through the leaders of the Church and leaders of the nation. If the devil can take the heart and soul of a leader, he knows he can take the people as well. Weeks before the election, a tremendous spirit of witchcraft was unleashed in the nation. It was specifically directed at creating hatred and division through racism. Then that same spirit was bringing about death and destruction with the COVID. There was the demon god Moloch that appeared in the spirit, commanding that we bow to him. The same demon was praising the work of COVID in the world. It was also declaring a "new president," and naming of Biden. It was the same devil, the same voice of satan.

God has already spoken His choice of Donald J. Trump. The devil heard it, but decided to over turn what God said. Now consider that God said <u>this</u> was **"His Grand Finale."** This means that God is holding the winning hand in this game. He knows the outcome because Almighty God is holding all the cards. Wicked men think they have won, but mostly it's a bluff. God is not mocked, nor will He be. God said that His **"enemies are in place. It's a fixed fight."** They cannot win. God has given them mercy and time to come to their senses and repent. Woe to the man who thinks God is a fool. The wrath of God is set against the wicked if they don't repent. We are in the days in which God will allow plagues and physical disasters to come as judgments against the wicked in this earth.

Until now, many have thought God to be asleep or nonexistent as concerning what happens in the nations of this world. They don't discern that it has been the grace of God that has held back catastrophes that could take the wicked out of the earth. But, we are in **"new era."** Jesus is coming back soon. Before He can return, all things must be returned to God's original plan. That includes all things both in the heavens and in this earth. All of creation must be brought back under the dominion of God's Kingdom authority. We are also taking back both the Day and Night for the Kingdom. Consider what would it take for God to overturn wickedness and restore everything back to righteousness? It would take a **"divine intervention."** We called it a **"divine reset."** Something so drastic has to occur that would cause powerfully wicked men to repent and turn back to God. This is where we are in the world. Therefore, it is essential, even vital to our individual survival to be able to discern good and evil. You don't want to be on the wrong side of God when the **"divine intervention"** comes into play.

We are at war for our human survival. God's people must discern the strategies and tactics the enemy uses against us. That devil is looking for <u>any</u> weakness in us. When he finds it, he will use it to steal, kill and destroy us and our destinies. To keep from being devoured we must not only know good from evil, but endeavor to do good and not evil. There is nothing so sad as one of God's children being used by the enemy to his or her own detriment. It often happens because certain people may be blinded by their personal pains and sufferings of the past. Offense is a trigger that causes people to operate in their flesh. *"Now the works of the flesh are manifest, which are [these]; Adultery, fornication, uncleanness, lasciviousness, Idolatry, witchcraft, hatred, variance, emulations, wrath, strife, seditions, heresies, Envyings, murders, drunkenness, revellings, and such like: of the which I tell you before, as I have also told [you] in time past, that they which do such things shall not inherit the kingdom of God (Galatians 5:19-21)."* Think about all of these things. Many people leave the things of God and operate in the flesh because of the perception that someone or something has hurt them, or deprived them of something they feel that they deserve. Instead of going to God and walking in power, they react in fear which causes them to walk in the flesh and not in the spirit. This is how many find themselves operating in witchcraft. When we operate in the flesh (our emotions, intellect, will) we have stepped outside of the covering of the Blessing, and have opened the door for the curse. As Jeremiah 17:5 says, *"Thus saith the LORD; Cursed [be] the man that trusteth in man, and maketh flesh his arm, and whose heart departeth from the LORD."* This is an area where our discernment will be in err. People will operate by their emotions and not by the Spirit of God. Remember that there are only two spirits; God's and the devil's. The gifts of God are without repentance (Romans 11:29). You will continue to operate, but under a different spirit. This is why we are told to test the spirits to see if they are of god (I John 4:1). The gifts of God will operate regardless of the spirit that is operating within you. If you prophesied under God's anointing. Then if you get into your flesh, prophecy will come forth but it will come out of one's flesh and not from the Spirit of God.

False prophecies come from those who have an agenda that has nothing to do with God's will. It's not so much about the words as it is about the spirit from which the vessel is speaking. If we want to keep our vessel pure for God's use, we have to crucify the flesh daily and submit to the Father's will. Even to know what God requires and not do it, this is sin (James 4:17). Sin makes us prey for the devil. God will never leave us nor forsake us, but we may leave Him in order to revel in our sin, in pride or rebellion. *"We know that whosoever is born of God sinneth not; but he that is begotten of God keepeth himself, and that wicked one toucheth him not* (I John 5:18)." If we walk in the truth of God's word, then that devil will have no place in us. Our discernment will then be aligned with the Father and what we speak will from Him. It is serious business to operate in the *prophetic*. When one receives a word, a vision or a dream, the first thing to do is to pray and ask, "God is this you?" I ask the Holy Spirit to explain what I had just heard. I will also for a scripture. Now, I have seen and heard some crazy things that made me question the Lord, but He always confirms His word. God may not always speak in King James English, but the prophecy will always line up with His word, and His will for the earth. The details may not be in the Bible, but if the prophecy is consistent with the character and nature of God, you can be almost sure it is from Him. Wait for confirmation, and instruction as to whether you are to speak what you have heard. Pray about it. Don't share it unless, and until the Father tells who to tell and how to share it with them.

Finally, there is one very vital area of discernment that we need to discuss. It is one thing to discern good and evil. It is another thing to be able to discern the Lord's Body. The Apostle Paul talks about this as it relates to those who take the holy communion *"unworthily,"* not taking seriously the sacrifice Jesus made for our redemption. *"Wherefore whosoever shall eat this bread, and drink this cup of the Lord, unworthily, shall be guilty of the body and blood of the Lord* (I Corinthians 11:27)." This a serious offense against our Lord. Everything we believe as Christians is based upon what Jesus suffered to redeemed us back to the Father.

Jesus demonstrated the holy communion for us to follow. *"And he took bread, and gave thanks, and brake [it], and gave unto them, saying, This is my body which is given for you: this do in remembrance of me. Likewise also the cup after supper, saying, This cup [is] the new testament in my blood, which is shed for you* (Luke 22:19-20)." The word communion is significant. It is the Greek word *"Koinōnia"*[2] which mean fellowship, or partnership. As believers, we are partakers with Christ in His suffering, burial and resurrection. That is why we are called, the Body of Christ. He died for all, so that we could take on His nature and live for Him. When we take communion, we are taking the benefits of the suffering and crucifixion of Jesus. His body was broken, so that healing could come upon us, His Body. He died on the cross, so that we, His Body could live in righteousness before the Father as sons of God. Jesus resurrected as the first be-

---

2   "G2842 - koinōnia - Strong's Greek Lexicon (KJV)." Blue Letter Bible. Web. 9 Feb, 2021. <https://www.blueletterbible.org//lang/lexicon/lexicon.cfm?Strongs=G2842&t=KJV>.

gotten of the grave, so that we, His Body would also have a bodily resurrection in the age to come. The holy communion is to remind us of all of these wonderful things the Father prepared through the sacrifice of the Son. To take communion *"unworthily"* is to mock both the Father and the Son, which makes us guilty of murdering Jesus. The Apostle Paul tells us the results of such behavior. *"For this cause many are weak and sickly among you, and many sleep* (I Corinthians 11:30)."* This is why many Christians are sick and dying. They do not honor the holy communion and the covenant God made with Jesus. Hold that thought. The Holy Spirit also gave me a revelation of how taking communion is a powerful defense against sickness and death. He taught me to take communion daily. It is the best protection for those who walk in faith concerning COVID. There is supernatural healing and deliverance in the act of taking communion and remembering what our Lord suffered for our benefit. Many days, I was in vicious warfare and the Lord would say to me, **"Remember the covenant."** I would stop and take communion and remember what Jesus went through on my behalf. The results of taking communion are supernatural. I cannot explain it. I just know that it works.

The Holy Spirit also revealed to me some years ago, that many in the Body of Christ, are also sick and dying because they do not discern and honor God's anointed leadership. People rebel against leadership. They murmur and complain instead of repenting and praying for leaders. We saw what happened in the wilderness when the people came up against Moses. His sister Miriam was afflicted with leprosy (Numbers 12). His brother Aaron ended up dead (Numbers 20:23-29). The men of Korah who rebelled against Moses' leadership were swallowed up as the ground opened up before them (Numbers 16). We saw what happened to Abimelech when he took Abraham's wife Sarah, to be his own wife. God came to him in a dream and announced that the king was a *"Dead man."* God also shut up the wombs of every female in Abimelech's house, *"for Sarah's sake* (Genesis 20)." The Psalmist wrote, *"He suffered no man to do them wrong: yea, he reproved kings for their sakes; [Saying], Touch not mine anointed, and do my prophets no harm* (Psalm 105:14-15)."* This is serious business with God. In the Book of Acts (Chapter 5), the Holy Spirit was doing many signs and wonders through the apostles, <u>after</u> Ananias and his wife Sapphira dropped dead in church. The Bible says, *"And great fear came upon all the church, and upon as many as heard these things."* Take note my people, because this is where we are in this **"new era."** The Church was in godly fear, yet the leaders were *"filled with indignation."* They seized the apostles and had them arrested. The angel of the Lord came by Night and brought the apostles out of prison and told them, *"Go, stand and speak in the temple to the people all the words of this life* (Acts 5:19-20).*"* The apostles were seized again and brought before the council. The high priest said to them, *"Did not we straitly command you that ye should not teach in this name? And, behold, ye have filled Jerusalem with your doctrine, and intend to bring this man's blood upon us."* Then Peter and the apostles responded, *"We ought to obey God rather than men."*

Peter began to preach Jesus. The Bible said that when the leaders heard it, *"They were cut to the heart, and took counsel to slay them* (Acts 5:27-33).*"* Then one of the council stood up, a Pharisee named Gamaliel. The Bible says that he was a *doctor of the law, had in reputation among all the people, and commanded to put the apostles forth a little space And said unto them, Ye men of Israel, take heed to yourselves what ye intend to do as touching these men."* Gamaliel began to tell of Theudas and Judas of Galilee who gathered together men to come against the apostles, and some were killed while others scattered. He concluded, *"And now I say unto you, Refrain from these men, and let them alone: for if this counsel or this work be of men, it will come to nought: But if it be of God, ye cannot overthrow it; lest haply ye be found even to fight against God* (Acts 5:34-39).*"* The council agreed with Gamaliel, <u>but</u> they beat them and commanded them once again, not to preach in the Name of Jesus. The apostles walked away from that beating *"rejoicing"* that you were *"worthy"* to be persecuted and suffer *"shame?"* The true believer in Jesus Christ will come face to face with this type of persecution in these last days. The persecution we have heard about in foreign lands has been rearing its ugly head in America.

There are many of us who are being persecuting in ways that would shock the world. For the safety of family and friends, we keep silent about our afflictions. We share only with those whom we discern are called to support us in prayer and spiritual encouragement.

The thing about persecution is this. Most people don't understand why they hate you. They just do. These are demons on assignment. It's part of the warfare of being called by God. The devil will use people to hurt you, to offend you, to kill you, but it's all for one end. He wants to stop God's plan and destiny for your life. That is why God's covenant promise includes a **"protection clause."** He Blessed Abraham saying, *"I will bless them that bless thee, and curse him that curseth thee* (Genesis 12:3)." God is serious about you not touching His anointed. If you want to stay alive and well in these last days, don't do or say anything evil about God's anointed.

I have to say one last thing before closing this subject. This is something I know in the deepest part of my spirit. Many people will be stricken with sickness and death because they have plotted and schemed against God's people. I am one such person. God told me years ago that He and I were in agreement to carry out His will. The Lord warned that there would be men who would attempt to divert me and try to destroy me in order to keep me from following God. The Lord promised to **"shake them"** loose from me. If they didn't stop, God said He would **"shake them again."** If they still did not let me go, God promised to **"remove from the earth (dead)."** You don't want to get in the way of anyone who is in agreement with God. We're not perfect, just determined to obey the Master. Another such person, is, President Donald J. Trump. You don't have to like him or his manner of speech. He is God's anointed. Take care how you handle the man. He is anointed to lead America in this current season. Heed the word of the Lord. Discern truth!

Waging A Warfare

Thus far we have learned that Jesus gave His people power to tread upon <u>all</u> the power of the enemy. We now know our God and our covenant with Him and Jesus Christ. We are ready to exercise our covenant rights and privileges. We know how to discern truth from deception. We've identified clearly that we are on God's side, which ensures that we have the victory. So, what are we waiting for? It's time to make tracks on that devil's head!

We're going to war against the devil as the mighty army of the Lord. First and foremost, we put on the whole armor of God and go in the power of His Might (Ephesians 6:10). This is a spiritual battle using Kingdom military weapons straight out of the Lord's armory, and we don't go alone into battle. The Lord will send His angel before us to take into the promise. When we obey our Lord's instruction, the angel will take out all enemy forces that have positioned themselves against us (Exodus 23:20-23). What is the promise? It is our destiny in Christ. It is the place that our Father prepared for us before the foundation of the world.

Here is where we battle. God has told us to go in and possess the promised land. There are giants in the land. We must dispossess them and take the promise by force. *"And ye shall dispossess the inhabitants of the land, and dwell therein: for I have given you the land to possess it* (Numbers 33:53)." What God has for His people is already in the earth. There are squatters on the land. There is a devil preventing you from having what God says is rightfully yours. Deception is blocking the truth of what God has given you. For example, you are a child of God and citizen of His Kingdom. Therefore you have an inheritance in the land. God has restored to you, everything the devil stole from you and your ancestors, all the way back to Adam. It's already yours, but the devil doesn't want you to know what is yours. So, he leads you to a church where religion is taught, but nothing is said about the inheritance that is yours in this earth. Ignorance keeps you in the dark. Then, you get sick, even with COVID and the devil tells you that death is the result. That same Church, does not believe that God heals today, even though the Bible says that by Jesus' stripes you were healed (Isaiah 53:4). Healing belongs to you, but in ignorance, you let the virus take your health from you. Then you rely on doctors and medicine, ignoring the truth of Jesus being the Healer. The devil will siphon your money, take your health and leave you a pauper, all the while telling you that it is the will of God for your life. The devil is a liar. Why do you mock Jesus by calling yourselves a believer, when you really don't believe? Listen, according to God, **"anything that does not line up with His word is a lie."**

The *light* (truth) of God is being blocked by the darkness [lie]. If you are a child of God, then you are joint heir with Jesus of everything that belongs to God, (Romans 8:17). Anything that Jesus has, you have. Is Jesus sick? Then neither should you be. Is Jesus poor? Then neither should you be. Jesus said that you would know the truth, and that truth would make you free (John 8:31-32). Is sickness making you free? Then it is not true. Is poverty making you free? Then it is not true. These are lies of the devil sent to make you a slave to the darkness [evil] of this world. Poverty, sickness and death are not from God. The devil brings poverty, sickness and death to keep you from fulfilling your divine destiny. Now, if you are the enemy of God, sickness and disease will be your portion. If you are one of the wicked ones who likes speaking sickness and death on others, it will back fire on you if you touch God's anointed. Life and death are in the power of your tongue. If you speak death, you shall have what you say about God's people. Repent, because that thing will backfire by holy fire in Jesus' Name.

If you are a practicing witch who enjoys spells and charms and all manner of incantations whether for good or evil, REPENT. In this **"new era"** that thing will bring holy fire upon you. The devil will turn against you and take your soul in these last days. He is not your friend. Beloved, please get this. If you are working for the dark side, the devil will take your life. Hell will be your portion for all eternity.

That devil is a liar. He will make all kinds of promises to get you to do his dirty work. He knows what will happen to you. He does not care what happens to you, just as long as you help him disrupt God's plan for your life. Sure, you can kill someone, but God will raise up another. His Will, will be done, in earth as it in heaven. End of story. Horrible things happen to people who are hell bent on hurting God's people. Death comes upon them and their children for generations. Death comes upon their associates and their families. You cannot speak and plot the death of another and it not boomerang on you. Don't be a demon on assignment. Repent and let God Bless your life. Don't let that devil take your life. Repent. Give your life to Jesus. *"Say unto them, As I live, saith the Lord GOD, I have no pleasure in the death of the wicked; but that the wicked turn from his way and live* (Ezekiel 33:11)." This is a warning to those who willfully oppose God.

Okay, let's wage warfare according to the Word of God. Remember that the weapons of our warfare are not physical. They are spiritual in nature and they are of God (II Corinthians 10:5). We take God's weapons and wage war against that devil and his wicked schemes. **Our main weapon; the prophetic word of God**. *"This charge I commit unto thee, son Timothy, according to the prophecies which went before on thee, that thou by them mightest war a good warfare* (I Timothy 1:18)." **Whatever God speaks to your spirit is the promise that He wants to bring to pass in your life in its season**. It is specific to you, your family, business, community and/or nation. We call this the *prophetic* word because it comes, not necessarily from the Bible, but it comes directly from your Father in Heaven. Here is an example.

Jesus asked His disciples, *"Whom ye say that I am."* Simon Peter answered, *"Thou are the Christ, the Son of the living God."* Jesus responded, *"Blessed art thou, Simon Barjona: for flesh and blood hath not revealed it unto thee, but my Father which is in heaven. And I say also unto thee, That thou art Peter, and upon this rock I will build my church; and the gates of hell shall not prevail against it* (Matthew 16:15-18)." Notice that Jesus pronounced a Blessing upon Peter because he heard directly from the Father in Heaven. Peter was not saved. He was not filled with the Holy Spirit. He simply spent time with Jesus and was able to hear directly from God. We who have the infilling of the Holy Spirit within us have a much better covenant. We have a direct line in our spirits to hear the Father's will at any and all times. We are more than Blessed. Notice what else Jesus said. *"Upon this rock I will build my church; and the gates of hell shall not prevail against it."* Right there, Jesus is showing you how to wage warfare against all of hell. You just need to identify the *"rock"* upon which the Church was build. That rock is revelation knowledge from the Father in Heaven. In other words, **"if you want to prevail against hell, you must have ammunition [revelation] from Heaven."**

Jesus then, tell us more about how this works. He presented what He called, *"keys of the Kingdom."* Keys are necessary to unlock doors for entry. They are also needed to lock other doors to keep the enemy out. *"And I will give unto thee the keys of the kingdom of heaven: and whatsoever thou shalt bind on earth shall be bound in heaven: and whatsoever thou shalt loose on earth shall be loosed in heaven* (Matthew 16:19).*"* Jesus was saying that He will give us *"keys"* of revelation, but we have to use those keys. Whatever we allow on earth, will be backed upon by Heaven, and whatever we don't allow on earth will not be allowed by Heaven. Whatever we do, as God's kids on earth, Heaven will back us up.

Let's go back to the example of COVID. God spoke to me directly from Heaven. **"COVID is Dead!" "Before the end of the year [2021], COVID will be removed from the face of the earth."** This was a tremendous key of God's Kingdom that opens the door to healing and deliverance for the entire planet. It is a declaration of God's desire for our lives. Notice that it is His goodness towards us to remove COVID from the face of the earth. While many are using the virus for financial gain and promotion, God is declaring that **"enough is enough."** He wants this virus removed from the earth, never to return.

What if not all believe, does that make the Word of God null and void? God forbid! Jesus said, *"Again I say unto you, That if two of you shall agree on earth as touching any thing that they shall ask, it shall be done for them of my Father which is in heaven* (Matthew 18:19).*"* God doesn't need a majority for His will to be accomplished in the earth. All it takes is two. Even if no other human agrees with this word, I believe, and the Holy Spirit that resides within me makes two of us that believe. We are in agreement with the Father for COVID to be removed from the earth. We say, *"Thy kingdom come, Thy will be done (Matthew 6:10)."*

Therefore, I wage a warfare against the COVID. In the Name of Jesus, I bind you COVID according to scripture, as the Father has bound you in Heaven. The Father cursed you and called you **"Dead."** I agree with God and call you **"Dead,"** and command you to be removed from the face of the earth in Jesus' Name. Notice how I spoke to COVID and reminded the virus that it was cursed to die and be removed. Some of you may be shocked that I spoke about the COVID being cursed. Take a moment to remember how Jesus cursed the fig tree. It dried up from the roots and died within a day (Mark 11:12-23). The disciples were amazed that Jesus cursed the fig tree and it died. That fig tree dried up at the roots. Jesus said to them, *"Have faith in God."*

Notice that I didn't have to curse the virus. COVID was already cursed by the Father in Heaven. That is why He called it **"Dead."** I simply spoke what the Father spoke. I didn't speak my own words. Like Jesus, I spoke the God's words. Now, I expect that the Father within me will do the work (John 14:10). From here until I see the full manifestation of this word, I will thank God for bringing it to pass. And, when people talk about how the virus is spreading, I will continue to speak, **"COVID is Dead!"** When people talk about going to get the vaccine, I will continue to say, **"COVID is Dead!"** Even if our government becomes brazen enough to violate our rights and require that everyone be vaccinated, I will speak the word only **"COVID is Dead!"** God has spoken. Let the Church say "Amen."

Am I saying that people should not be vaccinated? No! You do whatever you believe God would have you do, but I will not voluntarily get the vaccine. I have heard the will of God. To get the vaccine would be a violation of my faith. If God said **"COVID is Dead,"** why would I turn around and get vaccinated. Either I believe God or I don't. Either

I walk in faith, or I walk in fear of what a man says. God forbid that I would walk in fear of getting a virus that God said **"Is Dead!"** Faith means acting like something is true, even before you see the results. You speak it because you believe it, whether or not you see it. If you can see it, then it is not faith. Faith is believing that God will do what He says He will do. I believe God. Period.

Now, perhaps you have gotten the vaccination and are feeling condemned. Don't be. Even if you too have heard that **"COVID is Dead!"** Stop where you are and repent. Then get back on your faith. You can get the vaccine and still confess that **"COVID is Dead!"** Just like you would if you had received a word of prophecy concerning healing in your body. Unless the Lord specifically told you to throw away all medications, you would continue taking them until you consulted your physician. Verify your miracle with the doctor's report.

This is how you wage a warfare with prophecies. Once you have received the *"key"* revelation, put the Word of God in your mouth and decree a thing and it shall be established (Job 22:28). Jesus also told us that we could speak to the mountain and it would have to obey. What is a mountain, but something that is impossible for human beings to move. BUT in the power of the Lord's Might, we have power over all creation. *"For verily I say unto you, That whosoever shall say unto this mountain, Be thou removed, and be thou cast into the sea; and shall not doubt in his heart, but shall believe that those things which he saith shall come to pass; he shall have whatsoever he saith* (Mark 11:23)."

To wage a good warfare, you must believe that God can do the impossible. God's word in your mouth, working together with the Holy Spirit will bring the word to pass in the earth. *"And being fully persuaded that what he promised, he was able to also perform* (Romans 4:21)." This is a battle for our destiny. Once we obey God, we are not responsible for the outcome. The battle belongs to the Lord (II Chronicles 20:15). We do our part, and God takes over and does the rest. In the end, we win. *"Now thanks [be] unto God, which always causeth us to triumph in Christ* (II Corinthians 2:14)."

In waging a warfare, like any military strategy, one must be able hear new directions from the Holy Spirit. God may have a specific outcome He wants to manifest, but His strategy to get there may be altered along the way. You must know how to **"move and shift with the Wind of God's Spirit."** As Jesus said, *"The wind bloweth where it listeth, and thou hearest the sound thereof, but canst not tell whence it cometh, and whither it goeth: so is every one that is born of the Spirit* (John 3:8)." People will argue that God does not change. No, He does not change, but His strategies do. The Apostle Paul tarried at Ephesus because as he said, *"A great door and effectual is opened unto me, and there are many adversaries* (I Corinthians 16:8-9)." More than once he wrote about how the Holy Spirit prevented him from going to certain cities (Acts 16:6-7). Even if the Lord sends us to a specific place, if you are not received He may tell you to shake the dust off your feet and go to another place (Matthew 10:14). Discern the season or moment of change, and move with the Wind of God's Spirit.

There will be times that you may want to leave your military post, but the Lord will prevent you from doing so. Not only will you have to be steadfast in faith, but also *"endure hardship as a good soldier of Jesus Christ* (II Timothy 2:3)." Suck it up and then power up! You are called to this. Anoint yourself with holy oil as a reminder of what our Lord has imparted to you. Then immerse yourself in the word. Increase your time in reading and confessing the word. Commit what you have read to prayer. Build yourself up on your *"most holy faith praying in the Holy Ghost* (Jude 20)."

If the enemy persecutes you or threatens your life, keep yourself in the love of God and praise your way out! Let the Holy Spirit put a warfare praise in your mouth! When Paul and Silas prayed and praised in prison during the midnight hour, God sent an earthquake and loosed the chains of every prisoner (Acts 16:25-26). Stay mindful of your covenant by taking communion on a daily basis. Remember the Lord's sacrifice, *"who for the joy that was set before him endured the cross, despising the shame, and is set down at the right hand of the throne of God* (Hebrews 12:2)." When you have done all you can do, just stand. Stand on the word. Stand on God's command and don't waiver. Pray for your enemies. Pray for those who persecute you. They really don't know what they are doing. *"Finally, brethren, pray for us, that the word of the Lord may have [free] course, and be glorified, even as [it is] with you: And that we may be delivered from unreasonable and wicked men: for all [men] have not faith* (II Thessalonians 3:1-2)."

Let's consider one final example. The Lord brought to my mind, the 2020 Presidential Election. This has been an intense ongoing warfare. God is requiring that His army take a stand against the evil that is attempting to take over the nation. Demon possessed men were attempting to sell America to the powers of hell. They want God and His people cast out of the country. Therefore the Night is no longer for slumber, ignorance or sin. It's time to be on the walls of the cities and the nations praying fervently for the preservation of the saints. According to the Lord, the 2020 Election was not about who was in the White House. The Lord said, it was about **"Whom America will serve."**

When the polls opened on Election Day, the **"Kingdom Reveille"** sounded. The Shofar sounded throughout the spiritual atmosphere. Almighty God made a declaration of war. Battalions of angels were dispatched throughout the nation. Angelic activity was so thick you could see a clouded mist in the atmosphere. Then in the realm of the Spirit the Lord said, **"ADVANCE!"** He said, **"The War of the gods has begun."** On the opposing side, there was much witchcraft in the atmosphere. It was so severe that is was like being in a pressurized chamber. The evil voices were speaking the name of Joe Biden. Then appeared several demon spirits. One donned a face of an African animal. At first I thought it was a hyena, but the pointed ears and long face were more like a jackal. Then there was a hideous demon god terrorizing people in the realm of the spirit commanding them to bow before him. When Biden announced his victory prematurely, that demon god began announcing that America belonged to him. In all my life of praying for elections in this nation, never have I seen such evil in the realm of the spirit. If it could be put on a movie screen, it would be a horror flick.

Here is where the warfare began for many of those who heard God announce President Trump's second term. God clearly said that He had won, so what happened behind the scenes? Here is what God shared. The prophecy of Donald Trump's presidency had been known since before he ran in 2016. There was a war between then President Barack Obama and then Billionaire Donald Trump years prior. Did anyone question the animosity between the two men? When Mr. Obama began his "Stop Trump" campaign, he had waged a war against God. What he was really saying was "Stop God." Mr. Trump wasn't the only person whom Obama attempted to stop. He intentionally target Christians who were walking out God's plan for their lives. Mr. Obama opposed such plans operating in the nation. The Lord said that Obama was **"*jealous of the Davids*"** that God was raising up in the nation.

The prophecies about President Trump were well known among politicians and Christian leaders alike. Mr. Obama saw what God was doing and devised a plan to STOP GOD. Don't get this twisted. It was never about Mr. Trump. **"*The 2020 Election was a crime committed in an attempt to stop what God has destined for the welfare of America.*"** In August of 2019, the Lord revealed that Mr. Obama had a plan to commit **"*treason*"** against the United States; that he was going to **"*exploit*"** African Americans to do it. The Lord also identified others who were part of this wicked plan of hatred and racism. The Lord said that this entire election debacle was Mr. Obama's attempt to change **"*times and seasons to bring destruction upon the nation.*"**

That's not God's plan for America. This is our nation's **"*greatest hour.*"** God has declared that He **"*would do with America what could not be done with Israel.*"** God is in the process of making this country **"*a Kingdom example*"** for the world to follow. Almighty God will be glorified in the United States. The righteous will rule and the people shall rejoice (Proverbs 29:1). According to the Lord, **"*Mr. Obama arrogantly thinks he can overrule*"** what God says or does.[1] Here is what the Lord also revealed. The spirit of Antichrist is operating in many

---

1   Matthews, Paula. "YEARS 2016-2019: THE KINGDOM ARISES IN POWER! The Spirit Of Pharaoh Must Die!" *The War Journal Volume III*. Atlanta: Spirit & Life Publications℠, 2020. 141. Print.

who call themselves Christians. We see that in both our government and Church leaders. They possess a spirit of manipulation and control, because they don't know God or His Son. We are in a similar position that Jesus experienced during His day. Temple leaders were in cahoots with government leaders for money and position. They were not following the Prophet of God. They were following the profit "for God." They were only interested in promoting themselves. Jesus always called out the religious hypocrites. They hated Him. They claimed that Abraham was their father, but Jesus let them know that their behaviors determined the identity of their father. *"Ye are of your father the devil, and the lusts of your father ye will do. He was a murderer from the beginning, and abode not in the truth, because there is no truth in him. When he speaketh a lie, he speaketh of his own: for he is a liar, and the father of it* (John 8:44)." So many politicians and government leaders in America claim to be Christian, but their hearts are a black as the darkest Night. They are pure evil inside.

We discussed discerning truth from lies. You cannot rely on what people say. Watch what they do. Remember that there are only two fathers of spirits; God and satan. People will mimic their fathers. That is why Ephesians 5:1 tells us to be imitators of God. That is also why Jesus said, they would know us by our love for one another (John 13:35). If God is our Father then we should look like Him. And, we know that God is love (I John 4:8). We should walk in the truth of God, not in the lust of the flesh, which is of the devil. When God said that America was in a **"strong delusion"** it meant that we were following after satan, even by listening to and following after men who are possessed by satan. Blind leaders are leading the blind to their deaths.

When God revealed that our nation's leaders were warring against His destiny for America, He also said something very revealing. God spoke the names, **"Mrs. Harris, Mr. Biden, Mr. Obama, Mrs. Clinton."** What God said next shocked me. He said, **"The Four Horsemen Of Their Own Apocalypse."** I didn't know what to do with that information. I prayed in the spirit, but heard nothing else until later that evening. I had just climbed into bed and turned out the lights and the Lord showed me a *vision* that I had seen at least once or twice over the past several months. *I saw these four people standing back to back, as if to face off with someone. Then I saw military soldiers surrounding them. These were not American soldiers. The country was not revealed. They had weapons pointed at these four, but I couldn't tell if shots were fired. Instead, the "skirts" of these four people were lifted over their heads and their nakedness was exposed to the entire world. For whatever reason, the Lord showed the full exposure of Mrs. Harris. It was as though the others had pushed her out front to take the heat for what had happened in the nation.* After that *vision*, I heard the Lord say, **"It's over for Biden and Obama."** He said it once, and then repeated it. Then He said to me. **"Write it down."** I wrote it down and went back to bed.

The Lord also reminded me of something He told me back in the summer of 2020. The nation was in the midst of the virus scare. The Lord said that **"something more terrifying"** was coming to America. Immediately, He spoke about **"China, Russia, Iran and others having an axe to grind with American politicians."** He did not say these things to make me fear. No! It was quite the opposite. God spoke these things to make me aware. He told me to write them down in this book to make the world aware. But remember. God said that this was His **"Grand Finale."** He will be glorified in whatever comes our way. Those who align themselves with God will be glorified with Him. This will be a time requiring great faith in God.

Now, concerning the four horsemen. During the night, I heard, **"They will die in their sin." "My judgment is here," says God. "I have spoken My word and the evil ones refuse to repent. They come at My people as those ravenous wolves go after prey. As the day of My Son is near, so is the death of those who refuse to relent. They shall die in their sins. If they don't repent. They shall die in their sins and spend eternity in My Eternal Fire created for the devil and his angels of darkness," says Almighty God.** I got up wrote down the prophecy and prayed in the spirit. Then I read what the Bible says about the four horsemen. As I prayed and read Revelation Chapters 5-6, the Lord opened my eyes to see more about what has been happening in the earth. He revealed how the devil was using people to "wage warfare" against the prophecies God's prophets were speaking. These were not only prophecies about the election, but also prophecies about God prospering the nation and sending a wave of healing and deliverance to the nation. Just like God told us to **"wage warfare"** with the prophecies, the devil's kids have been told to wage a war against us; against us bringing the will of God to pass in our lives, in our nation and in the earth at large. We saw one aspect of this in the 2020 Election.

The true prophets of God were speaking what God said about President Trump's second term. They were speaking truth, but when Biden called himself the winner, many in the Church turned against God and turned against His prophets. They began saying that God couldn't make it happen, or that the prophets lied. They did not understand that we have to **"war"** in the spirit to see a prophecy manifested. We have to fight for the prophecies that point to our destiny in God. We saw it with Joseph, Abraham, Isaac, Jacob, David, Solomon, Jesus and so on. They didn't just walk into destiny. They had to fight. They had to wage a warfare against the devil. They said of Jesus, *"For consider him that endured such contradiction of sinners against himself, lest ye be wearied and faint in your minds* (Hebrews 12:3)." Like Jesus, we must endure hardships and persecutions on the way to fulfilling our destiny. We don't back down. We boldly stand on the Word of God. This is also why we pray for those in authority, that we may lead a quiet and peaceable life in all godliness and honesty.

We don't pray that one party or the other wins. That is not how God does it. Even though God chose President Trump, we don't have to pray that he wins. That is shortsighted. Mr. Trump is not the only one God has promoted in His Kingdom for such a time as this. We pray that God's will be done through all of those who are in authority; that we all can be elevated together. It's not about a man or a woman, or about any person. It's about God's will being done in earth as it is in heaven. It's God's will that all men be saved, that includes presidents, heads of corporations, judges, educators and the like. God wants everyone to be saved and come to the knowledge of the truth. There is one God. He alone is God. There is only one way to the Father and that is through Jesus Christ, the only mediator between God and men (I Timothy 2:1-5). God loves people, even our leaders. He sees their hurts and pains. Many are suffering. We expect them to be whole in their souls, but unfortunately that is not true. Many of these people have never healed from life traumas. Instead of healing, they compensated by going after status and position.

I recall a *vision* the Lord gave me about evil division in Congress. *I saw Nancy Pelosi and other leaders dressed in adult clothing, but God showed them as spoiled toddlers throwing rattles and objects at one another, yelling and crying to get their way.* These are the people making decisions about our lives. We **better** pray the will of God because they have sold out Americans to demons. The Lord showed me years ago, that the American people will be held hostage by our enemies. He said it was because of how the leaders of this country have conducted business over the past decades. He showed blood flowing from the top of the Capitol Building out onto the streets of the nation.[2] Our enemies are speaking death over America. The only thing that can save us is for those of us who can hear God, to obey Him now more than ever. We must wage a good warfare and stand for God's Kingdom to come, His will to be done.

The same night the Lord talk about the four horsemen, He explained how the devil knows what's in the Book of Revelation. He said that wicked leaders were trying to hurry the destruction upon America and the nations of the world. That is why they devised the "pandemic" and staged a coup to overturn **"the people's choice"** for president. God said it, not me. God keeps saying that President Trump won the election. Even while writing this chapter the Lord said, **"Donald Trump Is President of the United States."** Nonetheless, the devil is trying to destroy the president, the nation and especially Christians in this land. Here is the word of the Lord to me (January 24, 2021), **"I haven't changed My Mind. What I said shall happen in your life, in the Church and in America." "Write it down!"** Mind you that I am not asking God to give me a word about the presidency of the United

---

2   Matthews, Paula. "Year 2001: Preparation For War." *The War Journal (1999-2010) Volume I*. Atlanta: Los Angeles, 2010. 165. Print.

States. I have never asked the Lord anything at all about the Election or any of these people. He comes to me with these words and tells me to write them down. The White House has been my spiritual assignment for decades. Now, although we see evil leaders attempting to bring about the apocalypse, the book of Revelation records that it was not the devil bringing the evil. It was Jesus. He loosed the seals of the book in Heaven. That is how the horsemen were released. It wasn't done by any man in heaven or earth. No one was found worthy to loose the seals, but Jesus. Here is what the Bible says. *"And I saw in the right hand of him that sat on the throne a book written within and on the backside, sealed with seven seals. And I saw a strong angel proclaiming with a loud voice, Who is worthy to open the book, and to loose the seals thereof? And no man in heaven, nor in earth, neither under the earth, was able to open the book, neither to look thereon. And I wept much, because no man was found worthy to open and to read the book, neither to look thereon. And one of the elders saith unto me, Weep not: behold, the Lion of the tribe of Juda, the Root of David, hath prevailed to open the book, and to loose the seven seals thereof (Revelation 5:1-5)."*

Jesus opened the first seal and unleashed a white horse, that went forth conquering (Revelation 6:1-2). He opened the second seal and there went the red horse that was given power to take peace from the earth, that men should kill one another (Revelation 6:3-4). Jesus opened the third seal and there came the black horse to throw off the economies of the earth (Revelation 6:5-6). Then Jesus opened the fourth seal and there came the pale horse whose name was Death, and Hell followed with him. They were given power to kill a fourth part of the earth with sword, hunger, and death, even by wild beasts (Revelation 6:7-8).

The seals were God's judgments upon the earth. If Jesus is the only one worthy to loose the seals on a book in Heaven, how could Harris, Biden, Obama or Clinton to be the four horsemen? They don't represent God's Kingdom. Jesus didn't send them. They unleashed themselves upon the nation to wreak havoc, death and destruction. They chose to be tools of satan to do evil in this earth but God has another plan. These **"horsemen"** will become the victims of their own doing. God will not be mocked! They will reap what they have sown. These leaders have lost their minds if they think they can pull the wool over the eyes of Almighty God. They may have fooled some of the people, but the eyes of many are slowly opening to see this foolishness.

That devil is trying to bring this world to a destructive end. God won't let that happen, not yet, not ever. It was very revealing to me that the Lord Jesus only talked about the destruction that would precede His coming (Matthew 24). There is almost nothing good in what Jesus said would happen. However, there is a greater part of the script that has not been revealed in the earth realm. The Lord never revealed anything about what the Church would be doing, other than saying that the gospel of the Kingdom would be preached and then the end would come (Matthew 24:14). I get it now. My eyes have been opened to see God's military strategy. I see why Jesus never revealed any more about His glorious plan for the Church.

The devil can read the Bible, but he is not connected to the Father to know the strategic details. Since all the Bible shows for the end time is destruction, that is what the enemy is attempting to bring forth. Satan is attempting to bring about the events of Revelation, hoping to bring America and the world to a cataclysmic end. Imagine what he would be doing if he had knew God's complete military plan. Jesus spoke in parables for this exact reason. The treasures of the Kingdom *are reserved for* the people of God, those who truly believe. The devil's plan is to convince people that this is the end of the world, hoping that people would lie down and rollover dead. That is the devil's strategy, but God has another plan for good and not evil. We will see the goodness of God in America no matter which of our enemies show up to make war. God will use it for His glory. He will show His strength against our enemies, both foreign and domestic. The Lord explained it to me in general terms. He reminded me of His covenant with America. She is destined to be a *"sheep nation,"* with a magnificent inheritance in Heaven (Matthew 25:31-40). God will defend us, because we are a covenant nation. His mighty angelic host are waging a war against the wickedness of our nation. We, the people of God, the prophetic community of the Church, and those who are led by the Spirit of God, continue to wage war by speaking what the Father told us to speak in this hour. We have spoken God's word, and now the Father (through His angels) will do the work (John 14:10). It will be Biblical in proportion.

The Lord reminded me of how He handled the rebellion of His covenant nation Israel. It was never God's plan for them to have a king. God wanted to lead His people Himself, but they rejected the Lord their God and demanded to have a king like other nations. They wanted a king that would judge them, and lead them into battle and fight for them (I Samuel 8:7, 19, 20). Even after granting them their desire for a king, God let Israel know that they were not like other nations. Their covenant required that they continue to obey God, for their sake and that of the king. The same is true for America and every covenant nation. *"Only fear the LORD, and serve him in truth with all your heart: for consider how great [things] he hath done for you. But if ye shall still do wickedly, ye shall be consumed, both ye and your king* (I Samuel 12:24-25)." The Prophet Samuel reminded the people of what happen to their ancestors when they turned against God. Whenever they forgot God, their enemies overtook them. The people would cry out to God and He would deliverer them. It is the pattern of God and His people throughout the Bible. There was always a generation that forgot their God and fell captive to their enemies. That is the plight of America today.

If the Church has forgotten the God they claim to serve, how can the rest of the nation be blamed for not obeying Him? How can they believe on Him who they have not heard, or seen demonstrated in the nation? They have seen religion, but America has yet to see the gospel in its power. The Church has the assignment to reveal the Father to the world, but they have been following after man instead of imitating God. Therefore we are the generation in which Almighty God will make Himself known. Here is the thing. How a nation fares depends on whether God's people obey Him or not. The same is true for every nation that is in covenant with God. The healing the nation rests on the obedient of those who are called by the Lord's Name (II

Chronicles 7:14). If we disobey God to follow after a king, then God promises to destroy both us and our king. This is echoed in Jeremiah 17:5, *"Thus saith the LORD; Cursed [be] the man that trusteth in man, and maketh flesh his arm, and whose heart departeth from the LORD."* The issue in America is that the people want to be led by a man, and God is a jealous god. All is well for the nation whose God is the Lord (Psalm 33:12), but woe to the nation that turns away from Him to follow after a man. This is wicked.

The Bible records many instances where a wicked leader caused the people to sin against God. Here is one such example. *"Then the LORD will shake Israel like a reed whipped about in a stream. He will uproot the people of Israel from this good land that he gave their ancestors . . . He will abandon Israel because Jeroboam sinned and made Israel sin along with him* (I Kings 14:15-16)." It was apparent during the 2020 Election, that leaders were intent on turning the nation against God. Witchcraft was intense in the atmosphere, especially on Election Day. The people were under a spell. Many are slowing coming out from under the spell of the enemy. They are beginning to see the truth that was being placed before them. Regardless, God has made His desires known. *"For the rod of the wicked shall not rest upon the lot of the righteous; lest the righteous put forth their hands unto iniquity* (Psalm 125:3)." The Lord has spoken this scripture, by His Spirit many times since the election.

The enemy has come in like a flood over America. Freedom and liberty are at risk of being abolished. God is coming with a Rod out of Heaven to **"slay the wicked."** He will rule in the midst of His enemies and they will be struck down. *"The LORD shall send the rod of thy strength out of Zion: rule thou in the midst of thine enemies* (Psalm 110:2)." God is waging war with the word He spoke many years ago, when He said, **"America shall be saved!"** It does not matter that corruption has overtaken the leadership of the nation. It does not matters that the leaders of the Church have left the faith to seek fame and position in the world. It does not matter that the shepherds have abandoned God's flock and the wolves have made them prey. It matters not that the nation at large is deceived, confused and hurting.

None of this matters because God has a plan. He is moving by His Spirit even now to restore and heal the land. He is doing it through a remnant, **"a handful of believers"** in America. They are about to take center stage. The Night has spilled over into the Day. The darkness has been increasing upon this nation like a window shade that is attempting to block **"an even greater light."**

At creation, God gave us *"great lights"* to rule over the Day and the Night (Genesis 1:16). In this **"new era"** God's remnant <u>will be</u> the **"greater lights"** that rules over both the Day and the Night until Jesus comes. We are the Body of Christ, called to do *"greater works"* than our Master (John 14:12), walking in a greater glory than this earth has ever seen. We will speak (prophesy) to the darkness and call forth the *light*. Just like our Heavenly Father did at creation.

Sure, the enemy has stepped out of darkness into daylight with his evil, but it is no contest. He is boldly doing in the broad daylight the things previously done at Night under the cover of darkness. This is his attempt at **"intimidation."** God's remnant are not impressed. As long as the Church remains in the earth, darkness will not have total control. We will be here until Jesus comes. The battle will continue to heat up the devil. Get over it! We have a mission to continue the warfare and *"occupy until He comes."* We've heard the Heavenly command to **"Advance!"** We, the Mighty Army of God, along with the angelic hosts, will continue to advance and hold our positions until Jesus returns to wage the final battle for earth. The Holy Spirit said, **"Trouble is Here! It's a fixed fight!" "Hold fast to God's promise. This is time for the destiny of God's people!" "The Kingdom has come and trouble has begun. The enemy is retaliating but he cannot win." "It's a fixed fight, a set up from the very beginning." "God wrote the script." "We win!" "Walk in your destiny now! Your time is now!"**

In the meantime, the Lord continues to talk about what is going on in America. Recently, I heard something odd in the realm of the spirit. A question was being asked. To this day, I'm not sure if it was my spirit that asked the question, or if it was the Holy Spirit posing a question to me. In any case, I heard the following question being raised in the spirit. ***"If Donald J. Trump is the President of the United States, what is it that is attempting to take over the nation?"*** The Lord responded, ***"Works of men. It will be destroyed. It will not stand. It shall fall."*** It will come to nought according to Psalm 33:10-11. Shortly thereafter, the Lord brought back to my mind several things He had shown me several times before.

He took me back to the Night of Biden's inauguration. This was the first time Lord said to me, ***"Jezebel is in the White House."*** I wasn't surprised to hear this word. Jezebel is a manipulating and controlling witchcraft spirit. It's a lying, deceiving spirit that will stoop to murder in order to have its way. It's not only in the White House. Jezebel has an ally in religion. They both enjoy putting on a facade, and they both hate the prophetic voice of God. Therefore, the spirit of Jezebel can be found in many church and religious organizations. Wherever you find corrupt government officials, you will be sure to find them in liege with corrupt religious leaders. It is as true in our day, as it was when Jesus called out them. He hated religious hypocrites. He told the people of His day, to do as they say, but not as they do, because these leaders *say and don't do* (Matthew 23:1-3).

Jesus had a few choice words for these evil Church leaders. He called them, *"hypocrites," "child of hell," "Blind guides," "fools and blind," "serpents," "generation of vipers."* Jesus cursed these wicked leaders. *"Woe unto you, scribes and Pharisees, hypocrites! For ye are like unto whited sepulchres, which indeed appear beautiful outward, but are within full of dead [men's] bones, and of all uncleanness* (Matthew 23:27)." These are the same leaders who had Jesus crucified. Why? The people began following Jesus because of the miracles. Church leaders feared the loss of their positions and their political clout with the Roman government (John 11:48). Religious hypocrites love corrupt politicians, especially those who seek them out. This is what God has uncovered in America. When He repeated the word about Jezebel in the White House, this time, the Lord told me to check the script (Bible) to see what will happen to Jezebel. Then I heard, ***"Throw Her Down!"*** The spirit of Jehu is arising in the nation. That spirit of Jezebel (witchcraft) is about to be thrown out of both the White House and the Church house. God has only one way to deal with Jezebel. If the people don't repent, God will let the devil take their lives. It's severe, but the punishment fits the crimes Jezebel has committed against God and His people. She plots to kill the prophets, while deceiving the public into believing that she is a prophetess. This deception over America calls for severe punishment for those involved in this conspiracy against our freedoms.

On the day that the riots overtook the Capitol building, the Lord said to me, **"You have seen this before."** In an instant, the Holy Spirit, reminded me of a movie I had seen years ago. I didn't choose the movie, the television just happened to be on when the movie played. Sandra Bullock starred in *Our Brand Is Crisis* (2015).[3] The story was based upon an actual documentary by the same name (2005)[4] in which an American company was hired to over throw a government election in Bolivia. The media was paid off. Protesters were hired and the public bamboozled. Was the documentary accurate? According to the Lord, it really did happen. He said, that America **"Had done it before."** Now, we did it to ourselves.

So, how should we respond to such a *"heinous act"* that has been forged against America. Here is the answer the Holy Spirit suggested. **We will talk Truth. We will live Truth. We will stand up for Truth, and demand Truth from those in authority.** Jesus said, *"To this end was I born, and for this cause came I into the world, that I should bear witness unto the truth* (John 18:37)."

Pilate, the Roman politician asked, *"What is truth?"* The Lord said, that **"It is time for the Body of Christ in America to answer that question for the nation and for the entire world."**

---

3   *Our Brand Is Crisis*. Dir. David Gordon Green. Prod. George Clooney, Grant Heslov. Perf. Sandra Bullock, Billy Bob Thorton, Anthony Mackie. Warner Bros, 2015.Film.
4   *Our Brand Is Crisis*. Screenplay by Rachel Boynton. Dir. Rachel Boynton. Koch Lorber Films, 2006. Film.

CONCLUSION

Experience Good In The Land Of The Living

Beloved, we who are in Christ have the assignment of manifesting the goodness of God in the midst of evil. Goodness separates us from the evil, as *light* separates us from the darkness that is in the world. Evil serves to block the good, just like darkness purposes to block the *light*. God chose us out of the darkness, to take dominion over evil, with good. We are the *light* of the world. We are a *"royal priesthood, a chosen generation"* to show forth God's goodness (I Peter 2:9). We are the children of *Light* whom He called out of darkness of this world.

The LORD is good. His mercy is everlasting. His truth endures to all generations (Psalm 100:5). God's goodness, mercy and truth belong to those who trust the Lord. We war against the devil because we want to live the abundant life (good life) that Jesus came to give to us (John 10:10). We want to partake of His mercies that are new every morning (Lamentations 3:22-23). We want to walk in His truth. God's word is truth (John 17:17). We want to experience all the spiritual blessings that the Father has endowed to us (Ephesians 1:3). This is why we wage a warfare against the lies and deception of the evil one. We want to experience all the good things God has planned for lives, the thing our good Father prepared for us before the foundation of the world. We have a prosperous destiny in Christ.

We are learning how to obtain and sustain the promises of God. We are ever so mindful of the fact that the devil's scheme is to steal, kill and destroy what Jesus gave us. That devil uses manipulation and control to bring fear, pain, sickness, disease, lack and disappointment. He is the Father of all lies and deception (John 8:44). This is why the Holy Spirit commands us to **"Strive to see the good."** The goodness of God is hidden for the believer, not for the Christian, but for those who believe. There are Christians who don't believe the Word of God. They believe what they see with their eyes. They believe what they feel. They believe what the world tells them, what politicians and the media tell them. They believe their doctors. They believe in science, but they don't believe in God or in His Son Jesus Christ. They call themselves Christians, but they are not believers. How do we know? Watch what they do in the moment of crisis. Jesus said, that there are specific signs and wonders that follow those who believe (Mark 16:17). Jesus called out the unbelievers in the Church. He said that the *"fearful and unbelieving"* would have their place in the Lake of Fire (Revelation 21:8), along with the abominable, murderers, whore mongers, witches, idolaters and all liars. This is just how much difference the Lord makes between those who believe and those who don't. We are not talking about the world. We are talking about the Church. If those in the Church are not saved, what hope is there for the world? This is precisely why the Father is holding Court in the heavenlies and bringing His Justice to the earth. He must weed out the tares [fake Christians] in order to bring in the harvest.

This is another reason why we wage war against the devil, why we strive to see the good. The people of the world have not seen **the real Jesus** in action. They have no knowledge of **the goodness of our God**. It has to be demonstrated. Religion cannot, and will not demonstrate the Christ of God. They talk about it, but don't believe in it. Everything with God begins with believing. One must believe the goodness of God in order to receive it. David wrote, *"I had fainted, unless I had believed to see the goodness of the Lord in the land of the living* (Psalm 27:13)."* David loved God, but he was in a constant battle with his enemies. He could have given up and died. It was his trust in God that kept him going. David had faith that he would eventually experience the goodness of God in the land of the living.

David did strive to see the good. We don't know when David wrote this psalm, but he glories in the God in whom he trusts. *"The LORD [is] my light and my salvation; whom shall I fear? The LORD [is] the strength of my life; of whom shall I be afraid* (Psalm 27:1)?"* Listen to the boldness of David's words. The Lord is his *light* and salvation in this world of darkness. David was a man who praised the power of His God. He spent time meditating on what God had done for him. He knew the salvation of the Lord in times of trouble. David also knew that his strength came from God alone. This is the same David who, through his God, killed the lion and the bear. This is the same youth that, through his faith in God, slew the giant Goliath. As God's mighty warrior, David slew his *"ten thousands* (I Samuel 18:7).*"* He went from shepherd boy to King of Israel, not in his own strength, but in the might and power of his God. It was the goodness of God that David was promoted to king. David trusted God, but God could also trust David to shepherd His people with strength and love.

David encountered the battles of life, armed with the faith and strength of His God saying, *"Whom shall I fear . . . of whom shall I be afraid?"* He was fighting for his life. For every battle that was presented before him, David testified of his trust in God. He **"rehearsed"** the goodness of God. *"When the wicked, even mine enemies and my foes, came upon me to eat up my flesh, they stumbled and fell. Though an host should encamp against me, my heart shall not fear: though war should rise against me, in this will I be confident (Psalm 27:3)."* David knew the truth about his victories, that is was not him. David had confidence in his God.

We see why God called David, *"a man after mine own heart* (Acts 13:22).*"* You cannot go after someone's heart without spending quality time with them. David spent much time, in the presence of God, in worship and praise. The psalmist wrote, *"One thing have I desired of the LORD, that will I seek after; that I may dwell in the house of the LORD all the days of my life, to behold the beauty of the LORD, and to enquire in his temple."* The desire of David's heart was to spend time with his God. This is how he captured both the attention and heart of God. David knew that *"in the time of trouble"* the Lord would be there for him. He had intimate knowledge of the Father's love for him. David knew the Lord would set him *"upon a rock"* and place his head far above his enemies. This is why David could sing praises to God. He knew first hand, the salvation of his God. David knew that if he got in trouble, God would fight his battles. In this, David was confident. God loved this about David, so much so, that He covenanted to establish the throne of David's seed forever (II Samuel 7:12-16). From the lineage of David, Jesus sits on the throne of God today.

David reminds me of the Apostle Paul who also suffered many things for the cause of Christ. He said, *"For I know whom I have believed, and am persuaded that he is able to keep that which I have committed unto him against that day (II Timothy 1:12)."* Our Lord Jesus endured much suffering and shame *"for the joy that was set before Him."* He strived against the contradictions of sinners, holding His confidence in the Father's ability to bring forth the good (Hebrews 12:2-3). This is why we wage a warfare against the enemies of God. It is in order to see the good thing that God has promised. One must intimately know in whom they have believed. I believe God.

While writing this chapter, I heard these words in my spirit. **"You shall have what you believe."** Jesus said that we shall have whatsoever we say (Mark 11:23), but the faith process does not begin with the words we speak. It begins with what we allow in our eye and ear gates; what we see and hear. Faith comes from hearing (with the ear) and hearing (with the eyes of one's heart). **"Faith is in the eye of the beholder."** One must see [behold] something within the realm of the spirit, the deepest part of ourselves. Most humans only believe what they see with their natural eyes. God understands that about us. That is why He drops something within our spiritual eyes and then demonstrates that very thing before our natural eyes. This develops our faith in Him.

God's desire is to manifest His goodness in our lives. David saw how his enemies fell when God stepped in to saved him. David saw the goodness of the Lord in the land of the living. God will also show you something things in the realm of the spirit; things that are part of our inheritance. He will not only show it to you, but God will also speak words and prophesy what is yours. We saw this in the life of Father Abraham. God said to him, *". . . Lift up now thine eyes and look from the place where thou art . . . For all the land which thou seest, to thee will I give it, and to thy seed for ever (Genesis 13:14-15)."* Abraham was childless and God was talking to him about his offspring. The man was old and his wife Sarah was both old and barren, yet God said to Abraham, *". . . Look now toward heaven, and tell the stars, if thou be able to number them: and he said unto him, "So shall thy seed be.*

And he believed in the Lord; and he counted it to him for righteousness (Genesis 15:5-6)." Abraham was a heathen and yet he believed God and walked into his promise. For those of us who are in Christ, we are also Abraham's seed and heir of the same promise (Galatians 3:29). We can manifest the promise in the earth and draw all men to our God. This why the Lord is releasing His goodness and manifesting His promises greatly in these last days. He wants to world to see with their own eyes, that God is good. People will treasure these things in their hearts, and desire to know more about our God.

God will manifest His goodness through His people. We are Blessed to bless all the nations of the earth. We have to be like David, becoming people after God's own heart. That means loving and treasuring what God loves and treasures. We should desire to know the heart of our Father, and let that become our heart as well. The Bible says that out of the *"good treasure"* of a man's heart, good things will come forth (Luke 6:45). When we delight ourselves in the Lord, He gives us the desires of our hearts (Psalm 37:4). These desires did not come from us. They are from the Father. He places His desires within our hearts. Likewise, the more time we spend looking at the evil one and his desires, those evil things begin to fill our hearts. This is the purpose behind witchcraft, to place evil things in your hearts, to turn one away from God to the evil one. How else could America succumb to a **"strong delusion?"** Remember what the Lord said.

The news media is brainwashing the public to receive viral infection and death. They are giving people images to establish faith for sickness, and death. This is evil. These media people have no idea that they have become servants of satan. They are narrating the script the devil wrote to destroy humanity. For this reason, the preaching of the "good news" of the gospel is vital in these last days. People need to hear good news to counteract the evil that is before their face. Jesus is the Healer. People need to know this. They also need to know that if we abide in the Word of God (Psalm 91), we come *"under the shadow of the Almighty."* Like David, we must know that God alone is our refuge and fortress. In Him alone we must trust. He will cover us under His feathers. Under His wings we find trust because His truth is our shield and buckler. Because we made the Lord our refuge and our dwelling place, *No evil shall befall us, neither any plague* (virus or epidemic) *shall come near our dwelling* (Psalm 91:1-4, 9-10). These and other words of faith come through our eyes as we read them from the Bible. They become faith in our hearts when we meditate on them. Surely, it is only a matter of time until those words of our heart will come flowing out of our mouths to manifest in our lives. Jesus said, *"For out of the abundance of the heart the mouth speaks* (Matthew 12:34-35)."* This is the process of taking the promise of God from the Bible, from the Spirit of God and bringing that goodness into our lives. You see it. You believe it. You speak it and you will have it.

It sounds easy, and in theory it is, but like all good things, they are worth fighting for. Therefore, it is the true believer who will fight against the devil to receive what is rightfully theirs. They will push back the darkness and walk in the *light* of God's promise. The devil plays a game of **"keep away"** with the knowledge of God's goodness. The glory is a reflection of God's goodness. One one hand, the glory Blesses those who are obedient. On the other hand, it can destroy those who are in rebellion against God. Either way, as the Bible says, *"The earth shall be filled with the knowledge of the glory of the LORD, as the waters cover the sea* (Habakkuk 2:14)."* Whether we are with God, or against Him, all eyes will see the glory of the Lord in this season. The glory comes to prepare the way for the King of kings and Lord of lords. It precedes the presence of our Lord and King.

We strive to see the goodness of the Lord because it is a manifestation of His glory. It signifies that the Lord is with us, that He is working through our lives. No matter what we experience in this present darkness, He will not leave our souls in hell; neither will He allow the holy ones to see corruption (Psalm 16:10). We are eternally saved from the destruction of this world. We don't fear evil because we are seated together with Jesus in the heavenly places at the right hand of the Father (Ephesians 2:6). The best place of safety in these last days is in the will of God for your life. It's the place of both provision and protection. It's also a joyous place with endless pleasures. The Bible tell us that in His presence is the fullness of joy. At His right hand are pleasures forever more (Psalm 16:11). The fullness of joy? Pleasures forever more? **This** is *the path of life* that God has prepared for all who would follow Him. It is a path lined with all the goodness of our God. The strategy of the enemy is to keep people from hearing the Word of God. If the word got out that God is good, the devil would lose all control over the lives of men. Deception and distraction are his only recourse. God is good, and the devil knows it. He just doesn't want the people of the world to know it. As Jesus said, *"There is none good but one, that is, God* (Mark 10:18)." His goodness towards us remains forever. Even though evil came with the fall of Adam, God's goodness never left us. The *light* has never stopped shining. When Jesus resurrected from the grave, the Holy Spirit shed the love and *light* of God within the heart of every believer. God's glory resides within the believer (Colossians 1:27). The hope of God's glory is the desire of all His saints.

David declared, *"The Lord is my light and my salvation."* He was a man after God's own heart, but David was not perfect. He loved God perfectly. He was quick to obey and quick to repent. David demonstrated the goodness of God to Bless us in spite of what we have done in our lives. We must be quick to turn our lives back to God. This is another way we **"strive to see the goodness."** The enemy does not want you do see God's goodness, so he will keep you in condemnation and unforgiveness. He will always try to block the *light* of God's word. He knows that it's *the goodness of God* leads men to repentance (Romans 2:4). If you never hear it, or you don't believe it, you will never see it. It take much courage to see goodness when evil is staring you in the face. Darkness is ever present with us, but the *light* of God is ever shining, we just have to seek it out.

Until Jesus restored the Blessing to the earth, mankind could only live under the curse. This is where the enemy wants us to remain because it blinds us to the goodness of God. As the scriptures says, those in the curse cannot see good, when it comes (Jeremiah 17:5-6). The Lord has given us the Holy Spirit who is appointed to show us the good things that are to come (John 16:13), but we must employ Him. We must invite the Holy Spirit to show us and guide us to what the Father has reserved for us. The God's goodness is available to anyone, but His precious treasures are reserved for His family. They are hidden in a mystery. They are set aside for His obedient children. *"If ye be willing and obedient, ye shall eat the good of the land* (Isaiah 1:19)." Then there are other benefits to serving God in obedience. *"If they obey and serve him, they shall spend their days in prosperity and their years in pleasures* (Job 36:11)." Whether it is protection from our enemies, or pleasures and prosperity, or health and healing, God has special benefits for those who serve Him. *"And said, If thou wilt diligently hearken to the voice of the LORD thy God, and wilt do that which is right in his sight, and wilt give ear to his commandments, and keep all his statutes, I will put none of these diseases upon thee, which I have brought upon the Egyptians: for I [am] the LORD that healeth thee* (Exodus 15:26)." Serving God offers protection from COVID and other sicknesses and diseases. *"And ye shall serve the LORD your God, and he shall bless thy bread, and thy water; and I will take sickness away from the midst of thee* (Exodus 23:25)."

Love is key! It's the door to these and other benefits, because God is love. He wants us to receive His love and walk in it with one another. God created us in love, to be sustained and rejuvenated by His love. We were built for love. It's the stuff we are made of. The devil wants us to walk in hate and fear because it destroys humans from the inside out. The devil is a terrorist, a punk thug, who comes to steal, kill and destroy. Jesus gave us LIFE, beautiful, abundant and everlasting life. In Him is LIFE, and the life is the *LIGHT* of men (John 1:4). The devil's aim is to block the *LIGHT*, keep us from LIFE, and give us death. Devil wants to keep you in the curse by convincing you to trust man and not God. Remember that God is ONLY GOOD. Goodness comes from Him because it is a **"derivative"** of His Name. He thinks only good towards us. God is continually, perpetually GOOD. This is His love towards us. God will withhold no good thing from us when we walk upright before Him (Psalm 84:11). It is His good pleasure to give us the Kingdom (Luke 12:32). The Kingdom? God has given us His Kingdom! Where is it you ask? It is not something to be observed with human eyes. We cannot book a flight to visit the Kingdom like it were an amusement park. The Kingdom is within us (Luke 17:21). This is one of the mysteries of salvation. God's entire Kingdom is deposited within the heart of the believer. Inside of that Kingdom is all of God. He's in there. God is in us; all of His power and His glory. Imagine all God's goodness residing within your heart. This is the case, only if you are a believer. It is God's pleasure to give you all of His goodness. He is a good Father who gives good gifts to His children when we ask Him (Matthew 7:11). And, when you ask of God, ask BIG. He loves it when we have faith enough to ask for the BIG things. Then get ready. You asked for it. God will take you through some trials to prepare to handle that BIG thing. God has so many good things for His kids. The Bible says that *every good and perfect gift* comes down from the Father of lights (James 1:17).

God wants to do us good all the days of our lives. That's how much He loves us. When we return that love to Him, we can be sure that all things (even the *not so* good things) will work together for our good (Romans 8:28). No matter what comes our way, we know that God loves us and will only do us good. Then we look for the good to happen in every situation. It is a promise from our God. We are His children, heirs of God and joint heirs with Jesus to everything that belongs to the Father (Romans 8:17). It's all good!

God is our portion. We have a good inheritance. It begins with Him. When one receives the Father, He comes with gifts. We have gifts because of our relationship with the Father. It all comes from Him. It all is maintained by Him. For it all belongs to Him. *"For all things come of thee, and of thine own have we given thee* (I Chronicles 29:14)." We have a good inheritance. It is both tangible and supernatural, with gifts from Heaven that we can utilize in this earth. One of the promises of God that struck me when I first got saved, was Deuteronomy 6:10-11. God promises to give us, *"great and goodly cities, which thou buildedst not, And houses full of all good [things], which thou filledst not, and wells digged, which thou diggedst not, vineyards and olive trees, which thou plantedst not."* God does not give as man gives. He gives us good things and expects us to be good stewards. Yet, the things God gives us are not like those of the world. These are maintained by God Himself. *"For the land, whither thou goest in to possess it, [is] not as the land of Egypt, from whence ye came out, where thou sowedst thy seed, and wateredst [it] with thy foot, as a garden of herbs: But the land, whither ye go to possess it, [is] a land of hills and valleys, [and] drinketh water of the rain of heaven: A land which the LORD thy God careth for: the eyes of the LORD thy God [are] always upon it, from the beginning of the year even unto the end of the year* (Deuteronomy 11:10-12)." Since God is the one maintaining our lot, how can we tend it? Think about the garden of Eden. The Lord created the garden, but man did not toil to keep it. His burden was very easy. Man simply obeyed the Father and everything else was taken care of. This is how to live like Heaven in the earth.

God has always desired that we live days of Heaven upon the earth. That means not only longevity (everlasting life), but also everlasting prosperity, maintained by the Father. Adam didn't have to work for His wealth. His job was to learn of the Father and obey Him. That is where God is taking us in these last days. Jesus lived this way, and God took care of His Son. The Holy Spirit stated the Father desire for His kids. **"Take no thought for your life."** We are told to *"Seek First the Kingdom"* and God's way of doing things. Then everything would be provided for us (Matthew 6:33). These things are benefits of service to the Father. This is how we **"earn our inheritance,"** by learning of the Father, learning His thoughts and His ways. And, all things, even the entire earth becomes available to us.

The Bible says, that when we obey His voice, that the Lord will open His *"good treasure"* from Heaven, and give us rain in its season and blessing all the work of our hands. God even promises to give us so much wealth that, *"thou shalt lend unto many nations, and thou shalt not borrow* (Deuteronomy 28:12)." Let that sink in your spirit. God wants to open the Treasury of Heaven and bless you so much that you can lend billions and trillions to nations. And, you don't have to struggle for it. *"The blessing of the LORD, it maketh rich, and he addeth no sorrow with it* (Proverbs 10:22)." God is a good Father. He does only good (Psalm 86:5). He love us so much that He sacrificed the life of Jesus in order that we be reunited with Him, that we could live as sons of God. Not only did He die, but Jesus also took stripes on His body, so that we could be healed (Isaiah 53:5). He became poor that we, through His poverty might become rich (II Corinthians 8:9). Love is the key to everything that the Father and the Son have done for us. They gave everything, so that the Father could restore everything back to us. Therefore in Christ, all things are ours (I Corinthians 3:21). No good thing has the Father withheld from us. It all belongs to us.

As we walk in faith and trust God, these things will be released to us in the earth. We lay down our lives in response to what Jesus did for us. This is the greatest way to express our love. We honor His sacrifice when we present our bodies a living sacrifice holy, acceptable to God, which is our *"reasonable service* (Romans 12:1)." As we let the Lord lead our lives, He provides for us, restores us and anoints us to walk through the evil of this world. He rewards our obedience by Blessing us supremely in the presence of our enemies. We have assurance that His goodness and mercy shall follow us all the days of our lives (Psalm 23).

God Blesses us to be a blessing to all the families of the earth. Once the world sees the Blessing on us, then they will desire to know our God. The Bible says, *"And it shall be to me a name of joy, a praise and an honour before all the nations of the earth, which shall hear all the good that I do unto them: and they shall fear and tremble for all the goodness and for all the prosperity that I procure unto it* (Jeremiah 33:9)." Our Father is so eccentrically good, that He would lavish us with such abundance to make the world envy us. The Lord brought Isaac to mind. Abraham's promise on his son Isaac. The manifestation of the promise came upon him, but so did the warfare.

The Bible says that there was a famine in the land (Genesis 26:1-3), and God said to Issac, *"Go not down into Egypt; dwell in the land which I shall tell thee of: Sojourn in this land, and I will be with thee, and will bless thee."* Isaac found himself in a famine. God gave Isaac instructions [*light*] of how to survive during famine. The Bible says, God knows the way of the righteous. Their inheritance shall be forever. They shall not be ashamed in the day of evil, *"and in famine, they shall be satisfied* (Psalm 37:18-19)." Isaac went down to Gerar to

King Abimelech, just like his father Abraham had done in a previous famine. Yet, God told Isaac not to go down to Egypt like his father did. Egypt symbolizes the world system of doing things. God wanted to demonstrate the Blessing in Gerar, in a foreign land amidst strangers to the covenant. This was a set up for a demonstration of the power of God's Kingdom over the world's famine.

God said to Isaac, *"Sojourn in this land."* In other words, "Stay here temporarily as a stranger in this land, and I will be with you and will bless you before this people." Let me stop here for a quick moment. We talked about how we have entered into a **"new era."** God is doing a new thing in these last days. I hear the Lord saying that **"the solutions from the past will no longer work."** How we went about living will not work. Some may thing that it is because of the virus. Not so! God has been moving by His Spirit upon the earth, preparing for the return of His Son. Things have drastically changed in the spirit, we are now seeing that transformation in the earth. We will soon discover that the virus and other evil schemes were designed in an attempt to stop what God was doing in the earth. It will not work. God is in the process of directing all the systems of this world according to His plan. Again, God says that He **"cannot be stopped."** His enemies are about to learn this the hard way.

We'll will say it once more. God is good, and yet He prepares a table (filled with goodness) for us, in the presence of our enemies. The Blessing of the Lord makes us rich. Indeed the Lord does not add sorrow to His Blessing. However, we must remember how Jesus said, that the Blessing comes with persecutions (Matthew 5:11-12). In other words, the devil hates watching us partake of the Lord's table. As the goodness (favor) of God is manifesting on our lives, it will cause some to become envious and hateful. We see it in Isaac's story.

Now, the Bible says that Isaac sowed in that land during famine and reaped one hundred fold in the same year, AND God Blessed him. *"And the man waxed great, and went forward, and grew until he became very great. For he had possession of flocks, and possession of herds, and great store of servants: and the Philistines envied him (Gen-*

esis 26:13-14)." Obviously if Isaac had flocks and herds there had to be water in the land. So he was not affected by the famine. God had a plan. Isaac re-dug the wells that his father Abraham had dug previously. The Philistines were so envious that they began filling the wells with dirt. Who does that? The land was in famine. They had no water. Isaac Blessed the land with water. It was not only for Isaac. God had Blessed him to bless the people in that country, but envy caused them to stop up the wells they needed for survival. Are you hearing this? Something similar happened in America. God Blessed the nation under President Trump and his enemies vowed to see the nation fail before allowing the man to return to office. That is evil. That is also how envious the devil is when God Blesses His people. Watch what happens next.

King Abimelech came to Isaac saying, *"Go from us; for thou art much mightier than we."* Stop right there. Notice how the Blessing elevates God's people from a low stature to that of *"mighty."* Remember the mustard seed is the smallest (the least) among the seeds, but when sown, it grows up "mighty" providing for many. That's the power of God's Kingdom, and it will intimidate the devil. Nevertheless, Isaac departed and pitched his tent in a valley near Gerar, and he dwelt there (Genesis 26:16-17). Isaac dug again the wells from the days of Abraham.

The original promise and anointing that was upon Abraham, came upon his son Isaac. This Blessing caused much strife and contention with the herdsman in the valley. They believed that Isaac was taking "their water." In fact, it was the Blessing of the Lord opening the wells because of Isaac's obedience to dwell and sow in that land. Every time he moved, Isaac would dig another well and the people would strive with him, causing them to pick up and move again. Finally, Isaac went to Beersheba and dug a well. There was no contention for it. *"And the LORD appeared unto him the same night, and said, I [am] the God of Abraham thy father: fear not, for I [am] with thee, and will bless thee, and multiply thy seed for my servant Abraham's sake* (Genesis 26:24)." And he remained there and built an altar to the Lord. Abimelech came back to Isaac after realizing that the Lord was with him.

The king wanted to make a covenant of peace. Isaac made a feast. They ate and drank and departed in peace (Genesis 26:26-31). The Philistines realized concerning Isaac, *"thou art now the Blessed of the Lord."* Beloved, this is why we strive against the enemy. We want to see the goodness, (the Blessing of Abraham) in the land of the living.

God goodness extends to us, not because we are so good, but that God counted Abraham faithful, and Blessed him and his seed forever. We who are in Christ, are also the seed of Abraham called to be a Blessing to the entire world. We are called to show forth the love and goodness of our Lord. Even now, the Lord is revealing that the **"power of His Love is transforming the world"** as we speak. There are those who struck out at God's people in envy, but they are coming back to Him. One such group is the gay community.

God is calling the gay and lesbian community out of the darkness, with His love. He revealed to me the **"truth"** about the term LGBT. In the spirit, it means, **"Let God Be True** (Romans 3:4**)."** He also said that **"it was no mistake that the gay community chose the rainbow as their symbol."** It is the sign of God's covenant with the earth. **"They are coming in multitudes. They belong to Me," says God. "They will find the Love they have been looking for. They will find Me!" "Muslim brothers . . . they are coming . . . many understand Kingdom. The nations are coming in droves, even in a day!"** God is moving by His Spirit. The nations will *taste and see*, that the Lord is good and His mercy endures forever!

Life Or Death: It's A Matter Of Choice

The issues of this world are either "black or white." You are either with God, or against Him. You are either being Blessed or being curse, experiencing Life or anticipating death. Sure, it is not God's desire than any should perish, but that all men come into the knowledge of the truth (I Timothy 2:3-4). The choice is ours. *"Choose you this day whom ye will serve (Joshua 24:15)."* That is what God is saying to Americans, and to the people of the world. This is about more than being saved. **"It is about serving"** the Living God. We, His children, have been commanded to overtake the darkness of this world with the *light* of the gospel. We are called to preach (demonstrate) the Kingdom of God. This is how we will take back the Night from the powers of darkness. We must be about our Father's business while it is still Day. Yet, the choice is ours whether or not to obey. As the Lord said in the opening prophecy, **"those that didn't like the part"** He [God] changed. The Lord replaced them. Remember that He is the **"Director of it all."**

Thank God, that through Jesus Christ, we have a choice, but also consider this. The choices we make affect not only us, but our families, cities, nations and ultimately the entire world. Remember that God may call a man or woman, the their assignment is to Bless the nations. The Bible talks about how "one man's sin" caused the entire human race to be cursed. It took one man, Jesus to sacrifice His life so that we could experience the Blessing instead of the curse. God chose, one man, Abraham to impart His Blessing because He knew that the man would teach his children the ways of the Lord (Genesis 18:19). Adam had a choice. Jesus had a choice also. One man's choice brought the curse upon us all. The other man's choice restored the Blessing to us all, who would believe (Romans 5:12-19). All it takes for God to do the miraculous, is "one man." Herein is the mystery behind salvation through Jesus Christ, for indeed He is the only way to the Father. For in Him, has God spawn a new creation, "One New Man," within the Body of Christ (Ephesians 2:15). In Christ, there is no longer, Jew or Gentile, Male or Female, Black or White, Bond or Free. For in Christ, we are all one race, through the unity of the Spirit that resides within this new creation. For there is one God. *"One Lord, one faith, one baptism, One God and Father of all, who [is] above all* (Ephesians 4:5-6)." He is in all and through all. Jesus prayed that we all would become *"one"* as He and the Father are one (John 17:20-23). I hear the Lord saying, **"Don't be fooled by the 'so called' unity of the races, for there has only been one race that I have created, the human race. Unity, true unity can only come from Me for it is by My Spirit alone that I have created mankind and by My Spirit alone can mankind be restored back to Me. This is not the action of men, but the movement of My Spirit to restore all things back to Me, back to My original purpose and intent for My creation. I, Almighty God am The Great Equalizer. I alone can unify the race back into one. Watch as I move by My Spirit bringing all things human and nature, back to Me in this the last season of earth."**

This prophecy is right on time, because there is a movement in America that on the surface looks right, but the intent thereof is not right. There is a false move to unify the races, but it's intent is not to unify, but to keep **"scuttle"** among the people, and sink the American ship. The Bible talks about those who hate peace. They may even speak like they are for peace, but their hearts are for war (Psalm 120:6-7). These wicked leaders know that people's hearts are hurting. Instead of trying to alleviate the suffering, they stir the pot of disunity to keep things going. For decades in America, politicians have pulled the heart strings of African Americans. Wake up people, these wicked politicians don't care about you. They are jerking your chain as though you are a rabid animal they can control when they need an emotional appeal from the masses. This is evil, and God is putting an end to this **"showmanship."** **"Political racism has become so insidious"** in America, that people automatically fall into it's trap. It's no different from the days when White men commanded Black men to dance, they would dance. When White men commanded Black people to sing a song and they would sing. Politicians pull the chain of an angry Black man or woman and watch them react in ignorance, not even knowing who was guilty of a crime. Was it a government set up? Or was it a true race related crime? Was it real, or was it staged? Even Joe Biden had the nerve to brag about Black people being predictable in their voting. That should have been a clue pointing to their political strategy. But no! You thought the strategy was to get rid of Trump. Wrong! It was never about Trump. It was about using the Black vote to turn this nation against God. Period.

Your choice at liberty was stolen by what God calls **"a wicked counsel"** of men and women who **"sold this nation to the highest bidder."** The Lord has been dealing with them all. In the realm of the spirit, the Lord has shown His combat angels fighting the battle for the souls of Americans. Then I saw the Lord Himself dealing with leaders, including the Supreme Court Justice Roberts. It was terrifying to watch the Lord commanding Justice Roberts to **"Bow Before Me!"** The man refused to bow, but the Lord kept commanding, that he bow. The next thing I saw, he was on the ground. Not sure if he bowed, or if the Hand of God struck him down.

Beloved, God made His choice concerning our nation and its leaders. He has not changed His mine, nor will He. The Lord did say, **"China is coming! They will renege on every deal that was made."** They are **"fed up"** with our leaders. **"They will attempt to even the score."** Again, that is their choice. What will God do to protect America? Well, that depends upon the choices that we make from here on out. We rejected God once, will we do it again? The leaders of this nation have thrust us deep into the curse. They followed the path that Satan created for this nation. There is no turning back. This plot of evil must take its course. It will either break our rebellion against God, or sink America into the abyss in utter destruction. The purpose of the curse is to blind us from the good, to keep us in the dark, to keep us perpetuating sin and death. Thereby, leaving every American without a choice to live in righteousness, as God intended. Our leaders have chosen for us. They say, "Sin is in. Righteousness is out." The Lord came as **"The Great Equalizer."** Those who are born-again are afforded the choice of walking in the Blessing (righteousness, divine wisdom, *light*). The born-again person is established in the Blessing that causes one to prosper, when all others are suffering. The Blessing was God's original plan for all of mankind. It was the reason Jesus came to earth, to restore the Blessing to humanity.

Herein lies the issue. The people are accustomed to the cursed system of living. They have been trained to do and expect evil, and not to expect good. In fact, we have gained an **intimate** *knowledge evil*, and a disdain for that which is good. Hence we have darkness covering the earth, and gross darkness the people (Isaiah 60:2). The problem with the darkness is that *it is the absence of light* [knowledge of God]. It does not allow for *light* to come in. Those who love evil will attempt to put it out. Those who love the truth will come to the *light*, to make sure their works are pleasing to God. There is a way that seems right to a man, but the end of that way is death (Proverbs 14:12). Guess what? Death is not from God. Death is His enemy (I Corinthians 15:26). God never created anything to die. He's a god of increase, of multiplication, replenishing and subduing that which decreases. Sin and the curse brings about death, the diminishing and extinguishing of life. The enemy does this by keeping humanity ignorant about goodness, about God and His purpose. All deception is darkness. It gives people the illusion that they can live as they choose without consequences. This is a trick of the enemy. He would have people believe that God is taking away their choice. Not so! We told you that the Blessing of the Lord makes you rich, without sorrow. There is no backlash with the things that God gives us. Satan, on the other hand, is **"two-faced."** He will lure you to do his dirty work, then turn around and watch you suffer for doing so. That is why the Lord let us know that **"China is coming!"** Sure, they made deals with the leaders of this country, but China will be implementing their own plan. They don't trust our leaders in America. Any leader who sells out his own people to gain political power cannot be trusted. God is allowing our enemies to come against us, for His glory! Don't get this thing twisted. God is not saying these things so that the enemy can come destroy this nation. That is the enemy's plan, but God also has a plan that will take place in America. This is why God is giving us a choice to follow Him or not, with a caveat. *"Therefore choose life, that both thou and thy seed may live (Deuteronomy 30:19)."* In other words, if we don't choose life, then we nor our children will live. That means both spiritual and physical death and devastation. People don't like hearing that there are consequences associated with our choices. It's true nonetheless.

Listen. People want power to choose life and death for themselves. God has granted us that choice. The devil wants to take that choice from us because he wants power over the people. Likewise, the devil's children desperately want power. They believe that the only way to gain power is to dominate other people with threats and intimidation. This kind of power is cheap. It won't last, and when those being dominated decide to rise up, they will get revenge. The oppressed will become the oppressors. We, the people of God, have the **real** power, but most fail to recognize it, and therefore don't use it ever! Our power comes from our Father. It's source is the Blessing. When invoked, it causes us to *"rule in the midst"* of our enemies (Psalm 110:2). It causes us to reign in life by Christ Jesus (Romans 5:17).

God never gave us dominion over people. Neither does God dominate people. He gave us free will, yet **God is All Powerful!** That is why we call Him, Almighty God. He is much more powerful than satan. Most of the world does not know it. In America, the power of God is rarely seen outside of the church walls. There are even spirit-filled believers who think that God does not move outside of the building. Whenever they witness something spiritual moving outside of the church walls, many tend to believe that it's witchcraft. They don't seem to ever stop and think about what the Bible says. *"How God anointed Jesus of Nazareth with the Holy Ghost and with power: who went about doing good, and healing all that were oppressed of the devil; for God was with him (Acts 10:38)."* Jesus and the apostles were moved by the spirit and did great works, most of which were done outside of the temple. *"And by the hands of the apostles were* *many signs and wonders wrought among the people; (and they were all with one accord in Solomon's porch* (Acts 5:12)." If Jesus and His anointing is the same, yesterday, today and forever (Hebrews 13:8), why don't we see it in America? The people of God just don't believe that it's possible in our day. The Church in America **"has fallen prey to political correctness and bigotry."** Americans believe in religion, but not in the power of the Holy Ghost (the anointing that sets men free). *"And it shall come to pass in that day, [that] his burden shall be taken away from off thy shoulder, and his yoke from off thy neck, and the yoke shall be destroyed because of the anointing* (Isaiah 10:27)."

Religious practice only serves to put mankind in further bondage to sin. Jesus commanded that we be filled with the Holy Ghost so that we have *"power"* to be a witness of the resurrection (Acts 1:8). Salvation was always about *"power"* to change the circumstances of life for all of mankind, even to resurrect life from the dead. The anointing of the Holy Ghost is the supernatural power of God. When we obey God, the Holy Spirit does the work. Since so many Christians are fearful of the supernatural, the Church at large has developed bigotry against the Holy Ghost and the gifts of the Spirit. Therefore, religion is a result of darkness (ignorance and wickedness). It's one thing, not having a choice to serve God. It's yet another to make the choice, and then refuse to exercise that choice for God's highest good. Religion took away that choice for many Christians.

Before Adam sinned, mankind was free to make a choice for God without religious or political pressure. There was only God and man in relationship with one another. There was Zoe (the God kind of life) in abundance. There was no lack, no sickness, no death, nothing evil or sad was upon the earth. The Blessing reigned upon the earth. Everything was **"perpetually good"** for all of man's generations. If it were not for Adam's sin, mankind would have continued in that **"perpetual flow of God's goodness."** Adam turned away from God and caused the curse to reign in death. Darkness covered the earth, where the glory of God had originally been established. The darkness continues to take away mankind's choices in life. For example, the devil attacks at Night to catch people at sleep, to take away their choice. He is a thief, that comes to steal, kill and destroy. He uses witchcraft to control and manipulate people. Witchcraft takes away their life choices. It's playing god with the life of another. Our God is a jealous god (Deuteronomy 4:24). Jesus gave us back our choice to choose between righteous (God's way) and unrighteousness (sin and the evil way). Prior to Jesus' sacrifice, this was not possible. Our only choice was to walk in sin and all unrighteousness. *"For all have sinned, and come short of the glory of God (Romans 3:23)."* We were redeemed from sin and the curse by the Blood sacrifice of Jesus Christ, but that redemption must be received by faith. For those who receive Him, is the given the "power" (authority) to walk as sons of God (John 1:12). Even so, God will not force us to walk in His power. He gives us a choice. We can either walk in our own power (flesh) and experience the curse, or in the power of God (spirit) and experience the Blessing.

The matter of choice is always about power. Whom will we serve, ourselves, or God? We mentioned how love is the key, because God is Love (I John 4:8). Love does not force its way on another (I Corinthians 13:4-5). Satan, on the other hand, always forces his way on us. The tempter (Matthew 4:3) uses coercion, force, or pressure, and lust to force mankind to sin. That's his way of operating. God does not tempt mankind for any reason (James 1:13-14). That would be unrighteous. Love wants us to give freely of our own choice. Satan uses force and deception. He knows that mankind would be less likely to follow his wicked ways. He lures people to hell. Remember that satan, his demons and their witchcraft, are about being god in the lives of others. Satan wants to be like the Most High God (Isaiah 14:14). It's like Jesus said. That devil is a thief. He doesn't come through the door, he sneaks in through a window or by some secret way. No one would willingly let him in otherwise. Again, the devil attacks at Night when he thinks we are at our weakest to resist him. Even when he speaks it's all lies. The devil speaks, and it sounds true at first. Go a little deeper, and you will find the lie. He is the master of raising the question, *"Yea, hath God said* (Genesis 3:1)." That devil used the same strategy on Jesus saying, *"If thou be the Son of God* (Matthew 4:3)."

In other words, the devil manipulates truth so that people begin to question God's word. If he can get one to doubt God's word, then he can steal the word (Luke 8:12) and prevent us from receiving the Kingdom promise. Nonetheless, God's will shall be done by Heaven (Matthew 6:10). He offers each of us the opportunity to be part of His will. This is one of the choices God bestows upon us. Love always gives us a choice. It does not force His will on us. He gives us a chance to **"partner"** with Him in bringing forth His will upon the earth. This is why we get saved. The Bible says that we were chosen by God before the foundation of the world (Ephesians 1:4). He chose us and created us to be His *"workmanship . . . unto good works, which God hath before ordained that we should walk in them* (Ephesians 2:10)." Therefore, we didn't get saved to go to Heaven. We got saved to bring Heaven's will into the earth.

Think about this. Jesus defeated Hell, all by Himself. All it took was for Him to obey the Father, all the way to the cross. Granted, it was not an easy assignment, but Jesus had a choice. Yes, He did. Remember how He agonized in Gethsemane, before His crucifixion, saying, *"Father, if thou be willing, remove this cup from me: nevertheless not my will, but thine, be done* (Luke 22:42)." Jesus loved the Father so much, that He willingly went to the cross for our redemption. Love made a choice in our favor. Jesus defeat Hell and gave the power of Heaven and earth back to us (Matthew 28:18-19). *"As He is, so are we in this world* (I John 4:17)." We don't have to take on hell by ourselves. We just take up our cross and follow our Master (Matthew 16:24). We obey the word, the Father will do the work, which includes eradicating poverty, lack, sickness and disease, and everything that is under the curse.

Jesus came to give us back the choice to follow after God. On our own, no one seeks after God or seeks to do right (Romans 3:10-11). No one chases after God without being provoked. That is the way of human nature without God. Don't believe it? Take a look at witchcraft for example. Those who have no control over their own lives get their thrills trying to control others. These are heathens, wicked men ,faithless, unbelievers that the Apostle Paul spoke about. *"Finally, brethren, pray for us, that the word of the Lord may have [free] course, and be glorified, even as [it is] with you: And that we may be delivered from unreasonable and wicked men: for all [men] have not faith. But the Lord is faithful, who shall stablish you, and keep [you] from evil* (II Thessalonians 3:1-3)." This was a gracious way of letting Christians know that even while obeying God, evil men will come against you because they have no faith in God. How could they have faith in someone they don't know? Therefore, we as Christians have to have patience, knowing that if we are doing God's will, He will keep us from evil, for His name sake.

Faithless men want to take things into their own hands. They want to be the "masters" of their own ships, but they fail to realize that as a people, as a nation, we are all on the same ship. So, as they attempt to have their own way in the nation, they end up playing "god" with the lives of others. Did we not say that God is a jealous god? This is why He hates witchcraft. *"Thou shalt fear the LORD thy God, and serve him, and shalt swear by his name. Ye shall not go after other gods, of the gods of the people which [are] round about you; (For the LORD thy God [is] a jealous God among you) lest the anger of the LORD thy God be kindled against thee, and destroy thee from off the face of the earth.* (Exodus 34:13-15)."

Now, some of you might say, that's Old Testament. God wouldn't destroy wicked men from the face of the earth. Really? Listen to this word the Lord spoke to me back in 1998. It was a prophetic word concerning my call and assignment. **The Lord said that He and I were in agreement that I would do all of His will in this earth. But, He also gave me a warning that there would be men (wicked men) who would attempt to sway me to go their way instead of God's way. He [God] said that He would "shake them" to make them turn me a loose. If they did not let me go, He would "shake them again." If they still refused to let me go, the Lord said that He would "remove them off the face of the earth."** I heard those word directly from the Lord. Then a week or so later, I was visiting with a pastor whom I did not know, and God gave Him the same prophetic word. In recent years, I have come to realize that this covenant warning was not only for Paula. It is for everyone who is makes the choice to fulfill God's purpose for their lives. God is **"unstoppable."** When we become "one" with God and His purpose, we too become **"unstoppable."** Get out of our way before you get hurt. We talked about why so many Christians are sick and dying. They don't discern the Lord's Body. They don't honor and respect His anointed. We quoted the scripture before. I will say it again. God said in His word, *"Touch not mine anointed, and do my prophets no harm* (I Chronicles 16:22)." In these last days, we are going to witness what happens to those who refuse to honor God's people. We have seen it to a degree, but there is so much persecution against Christians in America, that God is about to avenge us all.

Here is an example, the media is very negative against Christians. Social media platforms are silencing anyone who has a differing opinion than what the powers are broadcasting. Freedom of speech no longer exists. That choice was taken from many Americans. These oppressors of freedom are serving gods that take away our choice to live a righteous life. Jesus died to give us back choice. Now, Americans stand by the choice to kill a baby, but the choice to prevent the killing of babies is not tolerated. They don't want to hear it. What about the young women who want to know the truth? Don't they deserve the right to hear both sides? Where is the choice in that? America's freedom of choice will completely pass away, unless we, the people fight for it. Otherwise, America will end up serving satan and losing all hope of prospering in her future. We've been looking to government leadership, without asking whom that leadership is serving; not whom they say they serve, but what their actions prove that they serve. Many are calling themselves Christians, but in truth, they don't believe the Bible. They believe there is a god, but He is not their Master. God is not the one directing their path. They are leaning to their own understanding and creating their own path, which will end in destruction.

The Lord called America's leaders the ***"four horsemen of their own apocalypse."*** In other words, they are the masters of their own destruction, and many Americans may lose their lives because of the decisions these leaders have made. Yet, God is watching it all. These leaders may be temporarily in charge, but God has the upper hand in this nation. Wicked leaders have attempted to take away the freedoms and choices for all Americans, by turning against God to do their own thing. Remember there are only two ways, two father's of spirits. One gives you a choice of Blessing or cursing, the other brings only the curse. You cannot serve two masters (Matthew 6:24). Going against Almighty God is not wise. You cannot win against the One holding all the cards. God is ***"The Blessed One forever."*** Satan can only operate in the curse. He is ***"automatically exempted"*** from the Blessing. Therefore following after other gods is the way the enemy takes away the person's choice of living the ***"Blessed life"*** that God predestined for all of humanity. The enemy makes an offer that seems to be one way, only to find out it was not what it appeared to be. It was a deception, ***"a spiritual mirage."***

America, whom will you serve, God or Satan? Some of you are so oppressed that you cannot see the way out. You don't believe you have a choice but to live the way you live. It's because you cannot see clearly. You are looking through a dark lens. Pray and let God illuminate your darkness. Let Him show you the way to freedom. You may be trapped in a turbulent marriage, or on a stressful job. You may be in a household of wickedness, and can't seem to get out. Pray and ask God how to escape. Whatever He says, do it (John 2:5). One word from God could open up a whole new world you've never seen before. This is what happens when God speaks to your spirit. He always says something we have not heard before concerning a situation. If you are saved, then you are God's kid, an "heir of the world." Don't let the devil convince you that there isn't any more than what you see. God always shows us something that we have not seen before. He will open our eyes to see the truth about what is available to us. With God, there are no limits. We can have whatsoever we say. But, how can you speak about something you have never seen? Abraham imagined his descendants when God told him to look and number the stars. Of, course, he never saw all of his descendants, but once God gave him the stars as a reference point, this enlarged Abraham's vision of his life. Don't ever let the devil trick you into believing that there is no more for you in this life, or that there are not enough resources to go around. This is a lie. Everything in this earth belongs to God. If all the silver and gold is His and the cattle on a thousand hills belongs to Him, what can't God get to you, if you believe? It's according to your faith, but you have to see it from God before you can believe.

Let's say it another way. The devil wants people to fear for their lives. Take a look at the world's economy. It is a **"fear based economy."** This was made clear during the so called "pandemic." People feared for their safety, for their health and for their financial future. Wicked men use the "pandemic" to control the masses. They used it for political gain, others use it for financial gain, while the people suffered. This is evil. It's also evil when men attempt to blame God for their dire circumstances. Satan tells men that God is the one responsible for sickness, that He sent it to teach them a lesson. Really? Then why did God send Jesus, the Healer? Why did He send His Word to heal and deliver us from destruction? Obviously sickness and destruction are not God's plan for our lives.

Some would be so bold to blame the Lord for their poverty and lack. They believe that lack is God's punishment against the world because of sin. You can choose to believe this, but to what end? If God owns everything what would it take for you to receive from Him? That is what you should be asking. "God, what do I have to do to receive all that you have planned for me?" This is the better choice, than sitting back and blaming God for all your failures in life. Besides, Jesus came to give us Abundant Life. God created this earth for mankind's enjoyment for all eternity. He created mankind because He desired to have **"a family on earth in whom He could give an inheritance."** I heard this directly from the Father some years ago, when I asked why He created us. Look throughout the Bible. From Genesis to Revelation, God refers to His people as, *"My firstborn,"* '*My children,"* *"Beloved,"* *"My son."* Jesus came as the Son of God, to restore to mankind back to the position of sons and daughters of God (John 1:12). God not only wanted a family on earth, but He also wanted to give us back this earth as our inheritance. Again we quote Psalm 2:8. *"Ask of me, and I shall give [thee] the heathen [for] thine inheritance, and the uttermost parts of the earth [for] thy possession."* Who are these His sons and daughters of God? According to scriptures those who are led by the Spirit of God are the sons [and daughters] of God. If sons, then heirs of God, and joint heirs with Jesus (Romans 8:14, 16-17). That is why the Bible says that it is God's *"good"* pleasure to give us the Kingdom. God says to His children, *"Take no thought for your life . . . For all these things do the nations of the world seek after: and your Father knoweth that ye have need of these things. But rather seek ye the kingdom of God; and all these things shall be added unto you* (Luke 12:28-32).

So, here is our choice for this life. We can continue listening to the lies of the devil and live **"disenfranchised,"** without Christ, and strangers to the covenants of promise, having no hope, and without God in this world system (Ephesians 2:12). Or, we can turn our lives over to God and let our Father take care of us. He promises to supply all our need according to His riches in glory by Christ Jesus (Philippians 4:19). When we choose to let God lead our lives, then He will take care of us from the abundance of His heavenly supply (riches in glory). Everything in earth belongs to God, but much of it has been stolen by the enemy. To retrieve what belongs to us, we must **"face off"** with the enemy by **"hearkening"** to the word [the instructions] of the Lord. When we obey what we have heard from the Lord, we cause His glory to manifest in that circumstance. The glory of God is **"His manifest presence among us."** Wherever God shows up, the riches of His glory will flow into our lives. It all begins with one word [wisdom] from God. This is *"sound wisdom"* that God reserves for the righteous (Proverbs 2:7). It causes a supernatural flow far above our human understanding. We obey God's wisdom plan, and **"the prosperity flow"** comes our way.

"I lead in the way of righteousness, in the midst of the paths of judgment: That I may cause those that love me to inherit substance; and I will fill their treasures (Proverbs 8:20-21)." When we make the choice to serve God, it causes all of heaven's resources to become available to us in our Kingdom mission. The Lord will daily load us with benefits (Psalm 68:19). This is the Blessing in operation. It is the power of God that prospers our path in life. Notice that the path is that of *"justice"* as we walk in *"righteousness."*

It's our obedience that allows God's abundant life to come upon the earth. We call it miraculous, but this is God's normal way of operating. His thoughts and His ways are far above ours. When He gives us His word to put in our mouths, it elevates us far above this world's way of operating. God's word to us is "sound wisdom" that will go from our mouths and accomplish what God desires. It will surely *"prosper"* in the thing where God wants it to go (Isaiah 55:8-11). This is the true **definition of prosperity**. It's not about money, or living lavishly in this earth. Prosperity may include these things, but it is not about these things. God's definition of prosperity has to do with the word flowing from Heaven, through His people to accomplish what God desires in the earth.

Let me stop here to address those who have mocked the so called "prosperity gospel." Do you want *"The blessing of the LORD* (Proverbs 10:22)?" Sure you do. People are crying out for God to Bless America once again. Why are people so desirous of the Blessing? It is so they can fail in life? What is the opposite of failing? Prospering. The world knows that God has Blessed America to prosper. So, why is it okay for the nation to prosper, but God's people [from whom the Blessing flows] cannot? The only reason America is Blessed is because the people of God in this country have made it their cause to preach the gospel to the nations of the earth. If it were not for the obedience of the people of God, this nation would have never been Blessed. Let God be true and every man a liar! God created man and the first thing He did was "Bless" them, to "prosper" even replenish the earth.

Here is the Bible definition of the Blessing. *"A blessing, benediction, invocation of good . . . the favour of God, the result of which is prosperity and good if every kind . . ."*[1] The Blessing is the favor of God that causes His people to prosper. It's a sign that God is with you. Remember Joseph, the dreamer? The Bible tells us that Joseph prospered because the Lord was with him. *"And his master saw that the LORD [was] with him, and that the LORD made all that he did to prosper in his hand."* Joseph was a slave and yet he *"was a prosperous man."* Even while in prison, Joseph prospered. It could be seen that *"the Lord was with him, and that which he did, the Lord made it to prosper (Genesis 39:2-3, 23)."* God prospers us with His goodness so that it can be seen. It's His glory on our lives. As Jeremiah 33:9 says, *"And it shall be to me a name of joy, a praise and an honour before all the nations of the earth, which shall hear all the good that I do unto them."*

Now, the Father gave me a strong warning to those who have put their mouths on prosperity preachers. **"Those who mocked the prosperity message will soon wish that they had listened. They will see it, but not taste it. They will be devastated by what is coming to America."** The Lord gave me a powerful scriptural reference (II Kings 6:35-7:1-20). There is a story in the Bible of a severe famine in Samaria in which women were boiling their children and eating them. The Prophet Elisha prophesied, *"Then Elisha said, Hear ye the word of the LORD; Thus saith the LORD, To morrow about this time shall a measure of fine flour be sold for a shekel, and two measures of barley for a shekel, in the gate of Samaria. Then a lord on whose hand the king leaned answered the man of God, and said, Behold, if the LORD would make windows in heaven, might this thing be? And he said, Behold, thou shalt see it with thine eyes, but shalt not eat thereof."* The famine ended just like Elisha said. When the people heard there was food at the camp of the Syrians, they stormed the city gate, trampling the lord to his death. He saw the prophecy come to pass, but lost his life, never partaking of what God promised because, He mocked the word of the Lord. Here is the word of the Lord to the mockers of the pros-

---
1   "H1293 - bərāḵâ - Strong's Hebrew Lexicon (KJV)." Blue Letter Bible. Web. 12 Mar, 2021. <https://www.blueletterbible.org//lang/lexicon/lexicon.cfm?Strongs=H1293&t=KJV>.

perity gospel, ***"the same shall be your lot if you do not repent ye this day, for the word of the Lord has gone forth out of my Mouth," says God. "And it shall not return to Me void. It shall accomplish what I desire. You shall see the prosperity of My people" says, God. "For it shall be a sign and wonder to the nations of the earth. It shall be a sign indeed, that I Am with these My Faithful children," says Almighty God, Who is Blessed Forever, Amen.***

God is serious about transferring the world's wealth and power to His people. Therefore, judgment will fall upon those who continue to mock the message of prosperity. You see, it was never about money. It goes back to what God did with Joseph, when He gave him instructions in how to prepare for a famine that was many years off. The plan for prosperity is about securing the future of God's people when the **"*storm*"** comes. Again, its like when God told Noah to build the ark because rain was coming. I'm sure the people around him mocked. They had never seen rain. Why would Noah need so many resources? Why did he need such a big boat? He has a small family. They don't need anything that big. You can imagine the comments, the laughs and mockery. They, like us, had a divine destiny to fulfill. Ours must be fulfilled before Jesus can return. Those of us putting together God's plan for what is coming, we have been mocked by family, friends and those who prefer religion rather than relationship with God. They don't understand, who we are or why we do what we do. They are not connect to the Father. They cannot see what we see. Nor do they hear what we hear. So, they make fun of us.

Let me tell you something. It takes great courage to follow God. It's not for the soft hearted push overs. You have to be strong and courageous to be mocked Day and Night, to endure the scoffers and the witches and demented people who are clueless. They have no idea that what we are doing will preserve their very lives. They don't realize that we take our assignments seriously because we see what the enemy is plotting against humanity. We endure the persecution and the name calling. Why? For the same reason we wage warfare against all the tactics of the devil. We want to see the goodness of the Lord in the land of the living. Plus, there is something we know that the masses don't have an ear to hear. God gave me this word recently. **"Those who mocked the prosperity message will soon wish that they had listened. They will see it, but not taste it. They will be devastated by what is coming to America."** Beloved, I have seen the cries of Americans who have not yet seen the devastation that is coming. I've seen the hurt, the longing and anguish of their hearts. I have seen how Americans will suffer if we don't build what God tells us. I have seen how those in the government are looking for power, but they cannot see the enemy's plot. Leaders are blinded by their own ambition and leading the people astray. It would be irresponsible of me to see the warnings and not to obey God. I'm working Day and Night like Nehemiah did, with a hammer in one hand and a sword in the other, because the enemy does not want us to rebuild God's Kingdom. He sends threats of death daily, but it is to no avail. God is holding me responsible for what He has given me. I have a duty to uphold for the Kingdom of God.

Here is the good news. Not all that the enemy is plotting will actually come to pass. God will hold back as much as can be allowed. America has a special place in the heart of the Father. Even the nations of the earth are in His heart. We all have a divine destiny to fulfill before Jesus can return. The word [prophecy] for our lives must manifest in the earth for the *praise and honour* of our Father. It cannot return to Him void. Therefore, prosperity is about the Word of God creating in the earth, what the Father desires for our lives, for our families, our cities, and our nations. This is **"whole life prosperity,"** which equates to God's idea of salvation. It's not only about going to Heaven. It is about living, happy, healthy and whole, as days of Heaven upon this earth. Prosperity means walking in God's *Eternal Life* the moment we receive Jesus as our Lord and Savior, not waiting until we get to Heaven. It means walking in the wisdom and knowledge of both the Father and the Son Jesus Christ. The more we intimately know the Father and Son, the more we learn about our royal status. It's an entirely new Blood line, a godly family with benefits both in Heaven and in the earth. It's a royal family of the highest order. God our Father is the King Eternal. In Christ, we have become kings and priest of our God, to reign here on earth (Revelation 5:10). We must choose to live the *Abundant Life* that Jesus offers us. This *light* that will capture the hearts of the people. Every believer has become a **"Light Bearer"** for the Kingdom of God. The *Light* of God [His Glory] is deposited within our hearts. The Apostle Paul called it, *"Christ in you, the hope of glory* (Colossians 1:27)." No matter what is happening around us, we have *"hope"* of something better to come.

As the world speaks death, dying and lack, the Father exhorts us to "choose life" so that we and our children may live in the glory. We choose life so that we can fulfill God's covenant, that we may *"dwell in the land"* which the Lord swore to give us (Deuteronomy 30:19-20). God has **"territory"** for each one of us to cover. It is a physical land. Do you think that God would promise to give land to Abraham's seed and that not include us? Consider who we are in Christ. We are anointed to reign as royalty in this life (Romans 5:17). Jesus told the apostles that they would be filled with the Holy Ghost and become witnesses first in their home town, then to the surrounding regions, and ultimately to utter most parts of the earth. Remember that God is concerned about the nations, His vision for us is **"global."** It is important not only to choose God, but also to *"go"* where the Lord tells you to go, for in that place you will be Blessed beyond measure, just like it was when Isaac went to Gerar.

God has a land [a promise, destiny] for each of His children. It's a *"good land"* that the Father cares for Himself. The glory of God will manifest through your obedience, for you are His **"Light Bearer"** in that land. It may appear dark and void at first, but when you go, you become the *light* thereof. You, Beloved, have the glory within you. You are carrying God's DNA in the earth. When people in that land see you, they will recognize the Father. God can manifest Himself to look like anything and anyone that carries His DNA [Spirit]. This is how the glory of God is manifested. It's the *light* of God in manifested in His word. The *light* [glory] is in the seed. When we act upon the word, it causes *light* to be released in the thing that God spoke to us.

Jesus demonstrated how this manifestation worked. He was strictly obedient to the Father. He showed us how to walk, and how to talk in this new Kingdom experience. Jesus was faithful to God, and His obedience changed the world around Him. He suffered through the darkness with joy. As He said, *"I am the Way, the Truth and the Life."* No man can manifest the things of the Father without following Jesus' example. If you want what God has, you must obey the Word of God. That means **"setting the atmosphere"** in and around our lives to reflect who God is, and who we are to Him. The enemy has no problem spreading witchcraft in the atmosphere. Why can't God's people set the atmosphere with His word, with His Truth and His praise wherever they go? Fill the atmosphere with good things!

Even people who join clubs and organizations fill the atmosphere with their joy. They will advertise by wearing a Tee shirt, or a hat, or even speaking slogans and joyfully sharing that "new thing" in their lives. How many Christians do you know that are doing the same? In America, there has been intimidation and persecution for doing so. Oh, you can advertise that you are a witch, or a satanist or anything that is contrary to God, but to actually stand up and be a **"Light Bearer"** for the Kingdom, it not so easily done without persecution. Therefore, it takes great courage to say you are a follower of Christ in America. You can go to church, no problem. The minute you stand up and voice what you believe, all hell comes against you, even in the Church.

What's the solution for those who choose Life. Obey God and prepare to be mocked and persecuted. Right now, religious Christians are doing that to prophetic, god fearing Christians. The news media and the world at large are also speaking evil about God's true believers. These have all made themselves to be the **"enemies of the cross of Jesus Christ."** This is a work of darkness coming against God so that evil can prevail in America and in all the nations of the earth. However, we must remember that God says this is **"His Grand Finale,"** which means that no matter what darkness comes, the *light* of God will manifest a greater Kingdom power and glory. Therefore everyone who chooses life must **"take a stand"** against the darkness. This does not mean rioting and threatening death as the adversary is doing today. It means sowing the seed of God's word in your life, in your family and in your home to demonstrate the power on a more personal level. It means enduring persecution and mocking. People do such because they don't know God, nor His Son (John 16:3). The devil wants people to believe that God is taking something precious away from them. Not so! God is attempting to give us *"the Kingdom"* which is the highest possible life on earth. God wants to give us His best in life. It's in the Bible, but until the people of God begin walking in it and demonstrating it to the world, it will remain only words on the pages of an Ancient Book.

Again, this is God's **"Grand Finale."** This is God's story, and He wins. Therefore, everyone who chooses to be on His side, is a winner as well. God will be awarding the righteous with great rewards in this season. The devil knows it. He is attempting to get as many people confused and out of order so that they will not reap their rewards. The devil knows the word. He also understands the times and seasons in which we live. We said that the devil's kids are using prophecy and fighting against what God is saying and doing in this season. They are attempting to **"foil"** prophecy and not let it come to pass. THAT'S IMPOSSIBLE!

Sure, the darkness had blocked the *light* in the past, but that was in the past. We are in a **"new era,"** a **"Kairos moment"** in which God's Will must be done in this earth. Nothing can stop what God is doing in this season. So, it behooves every human being to jump on board the **"Kingdom Train of Light"** because it is heading to a **"glorious destination."** God set everything in motion. There's no stopping Him now, not ever, never! The **"Grand Finale"** has begun. There is about to be a magnificent show of *Light, Thunderings and Divers Manifestations* of God's power in these last days, **"A Grand Finale Of Manifested Light."** Jesus is the *Light* [life] of men. His *Light* will manifest through us!

Imagine, God's word transforming your family, your business, your generation with *His Light*. One word from God can transform your entire world! This is what is needed to survive in these last days. No man will be able to prevail over the darkness. God is bringing wicked men to their knees in this **"final harvest"** of souls before Jesus returns. It will be a colossal fight to the finish.

Child of God, it's time we live by the Word of God, no longer by what we think, or by what others say. **"Come Up Higher,"** says God. ***"The time of man's wisdom is over." "My Kingdom has come. My Will shall be done, as I have purposed from the beginning, even before the foundation of the world. I Am God, I change not! This is My plan and It shall be implemented in My timing in this season. No one can stop Me. I Am the unstoppable, unchangeable God who has determined all things and purposed all things from My own grand design. You were not there. You were not My counsel. Therefore you have no say in what I do, only say in what you obey. Now go forth My people, in My power. You shall proceed and fulfill your divine destiny, In Jesus' name!"***

There you have it. We, the Kingdom citizens and members of the Royal Family, have been commissioned to show forth His praise and His glory in ways never before seen by mankind. We don't quite know what it's going to look like, nor what will sound like. We just know that it will be BIG. It will reflect the greatness of our God, and the vastness of His love towards mankind. He is taking us **"higher"** than any place we have ever known. He is drawing us **"closer"** to Himself.

Even now, we are **"setting the atmosphere"** for the greater glory to come. We are spending more time in His presence, listening, and obeying His voice. God is showing us a path of life we have never known before. It's a path of righteousness, that connects with God's justice, manifesting His presence where there will be the fullness of joy and pleasures forever more. This is *Eternal Life*. The Father will give us what we need to prosper and take dominion, in the midst of the **"ever resisting"** darkness of this world system. Darkness shall not prevail! We, God's Kingdom **"Light Bearers,"** are taking back the Night and subduing the darkness. We are not angry, just obedient to the word of God that will not return to Him void. God's Kingdom, *"shall break in pieces and consume all the kingdoms* (Daniel 2:44)*"* operating under the cover of darkness. They shall not stand, in Jesus' Name.

We don't fight with the conventional weapons of man. The weapons of are warfare are mighty through our God. This battle belongs to the Lord. He gave me a Kingdom parable as a scriptural demonstration of how this *Kingdom of Light* will be manifested.

"And he said, So is the kingdom of God, as if a man should cast seed into the ground; And should sleep, and rise night and day, and the seed should spring and grow up, he knoweth not how (Mark 4:26-27)." We, the people of God, are not only **"Light Bearers"** but also **"Sowers"** of the Word of God. We simply sow, sleep, get up and obey. We put the Word of God in the ground of our hearts at Night. We decree the Word of God during the Day. We don't need to know how it works. The ground knows what to do with seed. Therefore we sow, we sleep, we get up and obey. The Father that dwells within us will do the work!

For the earth bringeth forth fruit of herself;
First the blade, then the ear, after that the full corn in the ear."
Mark 4:28

Salvation Prayer

It's time to make a change.
Begin by giving your life to Jesus. Make Him the Lord of your life.
All it takes is one simple prayer.

Dear God, I repent for sinning against you and your plan for my life. I renounce satan, witchcraft, idolatry and all manner of evil. I want Jesus as my Lord. Cleanse me from my sins and all unrighteousness. Fill me with your Holy Spirit, and I will live all the rest of my life for you. In Jesus' Name I pray. Amen.

If you said that prayer and meant it in your heart, you are a citizen of God's Kingdom and a beloved member of the family of God. That means you qualify to operate as a king and priest for Almighty God.

Let the Holy Spirit teach you. Let Him give you the words to pray and speak. Let Him guide you into all truth.

Find a Bible teaching church and begin to fellowship with like-minded saints. Begin reading your Bible and letting the Lord minister directly to your every need.

Welcome to the Family of God!

BIBLIOGRAPHY

Matthews, Paula. *I Sought God And Met Him Face To Face.* Atlanta: Spirit & Life Publications[SM], 2020.

Matthews, Paula. *The War Journal (2011-2020) Volume III.* Atlanta: Spirit & Life Publications[SM], 2020.

Matthews, Paula. *The War Journal (1999-2010) Volume I.* Los Angeles: Spirit & Life Publications, 2010.

The Holy Bible Authorized King James Version. Nashville: Thomas Nelson, 2003.

www.ingramcontent.com/pod-product-compliance
Lightning Source LLC
Chambersburg PA
CBHW071848230426
43671CB00012B/2103